The Kingdom Has Arrived

Volume 2: Passion's Fire

The Kingdom Has Arrived

Volume 2: Passion's Fire

Snippets from a Wild Ride—A Prayer, A Poem, A Prophecy

Amy Jean

Jean Publications, Charlotte, North Carolina

Copyright © 2020 By Jean Publications, LLC

Library of Congress Cataloging-in-Publication Data
LCCN - 2019916443

ISBN - 978-1-7340430-3-7 (hardcover)
ISBN - 978-1-7340430-4-4 (softcover)
ISBN - 978-1-7340430-5-1 (softcover, color)

Copy Editor: Bob Cooper
Contributing Editor: Elizabeth Judd
Book cover and illustrations by Eric Savage
Photography by Amy Jean
Book Design by Amy Jean and Eric Savage

Dedication

This book is dedicated to civilized people, who, at the end of the day, make their decisions based on love. Life should not be lived by collecting belongings, property, or people as though it were a game. The people who understand that life should be embraced, are the ones who have a positive impact on their sisters and brothers. Those building God's Kingdom are the ones who stop and listen to you intently and then remember your life stories ten or twenty years later. They make you laugh, and you always feel better after spending time with them. They lend you a hand when you need one with no expectation of getting anything in return. They tell you the truth, even if it hurts, and give you a kick in the butt when you need one. They don't step on others to lift themselves up but instead bend down to help others up. They see what is lacking in the universe, determine how they will contribute, and then act rather than sitting around assuming someone else has it covered. They forgive you quickly when you make mistakes and love you in spite of them. In my experience, these individuals are rarely popular. They are unique, often outcasts, sometimes nerdy—but frequently they are the game-changers. They are the women and men in the universe who live and have lived their lives with love at the center. Lives lived in the present create beautiful stories and memories that make one's life and the lives of others joy-filled. They are the people I choose to surround myself with; The reason why is simple: Historically, they have the most positive impact on humanity.

Albert Einstein didn't speak for the first three years of his life. They say his head was in the clouds. Benjamin Franklin dropped out of school at age ten because his parents couldn't afford to keep him in school. Talk about isolation. Thomas Edison failed more than 1,000 times before inventing the light bulb. I bet he felt like a failure for quite some time. Vincent Van Gogh sold only one painting during his lifetime. Not so successful, was he? John the Baptist was a homeless man, wandering the wilderness, eating locusts and honey in between dunking people in water—need I say more? Padre Pio was silenced by the Vatican for years, then later declared a saint. Jesus Christ went to the desert, not eating for forty days, performed miracles, fed the masses, and the world crucified Him. Wow! Many saints and prominent religious leaders were considered mentally off. After all, as mystics, they saw things and heard things that others did not see or hear. Hallucinations? Or maybe they lived while the rest of the world was delusional?

Whoever said it was the climb
. . . LIED!

—Amy Jean

Contents

Illustrations and Photos

Preface

It's odd how life just moves forward after an experience like the passion journey I suffered in the mental hospital. Moving forward didn't seem natural to me because I was feeling the shackles on my ankles and the wounds of Christ daily, while revelation was flowing freely at me. Also, my sons and husband were acting differently. While they were in my presence, I felt like they had been taken from me. They were behaving as if they were on a mission they believed in but that I was not privy to—a mission meant to restore me. When I said anything to them to try to confirm my suspicions, they would deny knowing what I was talking about. How in the world could the sons I bore and raised now be tasked with a mission to raise me? My new life dynamic felt backward, and I hated the idea that they would suffer or watch me suffer.

My current situation reminded me of when Benjamin was in first grade. He came home from school one day sad because a boy at his lunch table sat alone and told all the kids that he was in a Star Wars bubble, which was why nobody could sit next to him. The little boy had greasy hair, dirty clothes, and emitted an unpleasant odor. While many of the other children teased the boy, it made Benjamin very sad, and he was teary-eyed as he told me about the boy sitting alone at the end of the table. I told Benjamin to share with the boy how much he likes Star Wars and to ask him if he could sit in the bubble with him. Benjamin did precisely that the next day, and eventually, all the boys at his lunch table were seated in the Star Wars bubble with Ben and the outcast.

I, of course, was a proud mother—and what mother wouldn't be with a son like that. But I had the distinct feeling that now my boys and husband were stuck in a bubble with me. And I did not like that at all. It seemed like Benjamin was trapped there with me more so than the others, primarily because I would hear his voice in my head from time to time, saying, "Mom, Mom, he touched me!" Ben was joking, of course, and poking fun at me because I kept saying in my dreams, thoughts, and even out loud at times, "If you ever touch my sons, I will hunt you down for an eternity, and you will wish you were never born." What I thought they were going to do to my sons precisely, I don't know. But there is no way in hell anyone was going to separate my boys or make them suffer this insane purification and circumcision that I am going through. NOT HAPPENING!

One thing that kept me going was the last vision I had when I was lying on the bed in the mental hospital after the locusts had lifted and libraries of information began pouring into my mind. I saw thousands of people in an outdoor open area like the piazza at the front of the Vatican. People were being rescattered into families or groups going in different directions. They were calling me a Zazzy Queen because I had been so fiery and stubborn to handle. I had a little Australian shepherd and was wearing jeans, a T-shirt, and swanky shoes while all the other queens had fancy clothes, fancy makeup, and some plastic inserted here and there as if they had signed up to be Barbie dolls. Don't get me wrong, I loved playing with Barbies when I was a kid, but I had no interest in being one.

I didn't develop insecurities until my first love tossed me aside. Then I started to wonder if I needed to wear fancy clothes or have bigger boobs. But I refused to become synthetic to please a man. I waited until I found someone who loved me exactly the way God made me. Once again, I was the outcast of the bunch at the rescattering. But I didn't care, because not only were all my boys together with me but also all my friends and family, including my mom and dad, who had long since passed away. And my sister was no longer sick.

It was a marvelous vision that keeps me going daily. It would most certainly be Heaven on Earth. And I am a dreamer, so I plan on dreaming until my dreams come true.

After all, with God, anything is possible.

A Note On Sources

Throughout my faith journey, I have used several versions of the Bible. This was partially because they were available when I was seeking a word from God but also because it was a part of the logical, systematic experiment I embarked on over the course of my faith journey. And sometimes, the slight variation in wording spoke differently to me or answered a specific prayer. The following Bibles are referenced in this book: NABRE, NRSV, NRSVA, NASB, RSV, NIV, CJB, and KJV.

Here is why I looked at so many versions of the Bible: I started to notice that the meaning of god's message changed depending on which version I was reading. How odd is it that sometimes the passage below reads "in the image of God he created him" and other times it reads "in the image of God he created them"? There are many other passages where one version would say "mankind" and another would say "humankind." In yet other Scripture passages, one version would say "man and woman" but another says just "man." Peculiar if you ask me. I write a story and stick to it. If I don't like that story, I will write a new one.

Genesis 1:27–28 New Revised Standard Version, Anglicized (NRSVA)

So God created humankind in his image, in the image of God he created them; male and female he created them. God blessed them, and God said to them, 'Be fruitful and multiply, and fill the earth and subdue it; and have dominion over the fish of the sea and over the birds of the air and over every living thing that moves upon the earth.'

Genesis 1:27–28 New American Bible (Revised Edition) (NABRE)

God created mankind in his image; in the image of God he created them; male and female he created them. God blessed them and God said to them: Be fertile and multiply; fill the earth and subdue it. Have dominion over the fish of the sea, the birds of the air, and all the living things that crawl on the earth.

Genesis 1:27–28 Complete Jewish Bible (CJB)

So God created humankind in his own image; in the image of God he created him: male and female he created them. God blessed them: God said to them, "Be fruitful, multiply, fill the earth and subdue it. Rule over the fish in the sea, the birds in the air and every living creature that crawls on the earth."

Acknowledgments

I am going to start by acknowledging Buck. Primarily because after twenty-eight years of separation, he agreed to meet with me and seemed to believe every word I said to him. I was believed, and that deserves serious acknowledgment regardless of what happens in the future or what he may have said or done behind my back. I also must thank Buck's parents because they listened to an outrageous story from their son's old girlfriend. They were kind and gracious while I babbled my tale as tears rolled down my cheeks. Thank you.

I continue to survive and tread my tumultuous path being held up by Charles, Benjamin, Jeffrey, and Nicholas, who are legendary rock stars in my mind. A special thanks to Sister Mary, who has supported me and made me feel important when I felt like a crazy mess. You are a sweet and solid rock.

Many thanks to my graphic artist and illustrator, Eric Savage, who not only created beautiful illustrations to go along with my story but made my book look professional. Finally, thanks to my editors, Bob Cooper and Elizabeth Judd for your attention to all the little details that pulled this volume together masterfully.

Introduction

Facing my truth is not something I ever wanted to do if I'm entirely honest. To admit that I had been hiding from my flaws, failures, and insecurities seemed like an insane thing to do so late in the game. Now in my early fifties, shouldn't I have figured out who I was and what I wanted? I had successfully raised three sons.

At this stage of life, to be contemplating whether I had made conscious decisions about what I wanted in life seemed ridiculous. And who wants to look like a fool in their fifties? That is when I should be bubbling over with self-confidence and not giving a shit what anyone else says or thinks. I should know who I am, what I want out of life, and be basking in joy daily because I'm comfortable in my skin. Right?

Instead, I was walking around feeling invisible shackles on my ankles, experiencing the pains of Christ daily, and hearing the heavens guiding me down an insane passage. Where the journey led, I didn't know, but stepping off the path was not an option. One alternative would have been to end myself, and there were plenty of times I considered that option, but I refused to do that to my sons. I didn't want them to go through life without their mother as I had. Plus, I believed what I heard Jesus telling me, and I was so in love that I didn't want to take any chance of not getting to Him at the end of the day.

SHARING LIGHT, LOVE, AND TRUTH

1 Lady Zion

To relax, I frequently go to Charleston for a weekend of solitude. One Saturday morning, I woke up and lugged my paddleboard down to the dock. It was a beautiful morning, and the birds and wildlife on the creek were out singing glorious praises to God in unison. All of nature seemed overjoyed with the progress of my transformation and were joining in the celebration of my Divine restoration.

As I paddled down Shem Creek, my eyes were opened to the abyss below me as I floated above the world, taking in a glimpse of the Master's view. It was not entirely a pretty sight. We, here on earth, are wrong and confused about so many things. However, many of God's creations were in perfection that morning. While people appeared to not want to interact with me, the wildlife did, and I was content communing with nature.

I paddled under the bridge and into the stretch of the creek that opens out to the ocean. Nature was out in full force, more so than I had ever seen in my lifetime. There were pelicans, manatees, dolphins, turtles, jellyfish, stingrays, and birds everywhere. The view was breathtaking. I sat down on my paddleboard, pulled my camera out of my dry bag, and started shooting pictures.

That Saturday, God's creatures were approaching me without fear; the whole of creation was funneling though me in a two-way vibration that reverberated in every molecule of my body. I was somehow one with the creator of nature and humanity. A glorious celebration like none I had ever experienced transpired—a moment of perfect harmony that is permanently imprinted on my soul.

When I got back to my apartment later that afternoon, I uploaded the pictures onto my computer and sat marveling at the images. It occurred to me that several of the photos I took that day corresponded perfectly with the Scriptures that I had written in my journal earlier in the week.

I added Scripture to the pictures and framed a series of seven.

The Watchmen

Hark! Your watchmen raise a cry,
together they shout for joy,
For they see directly, before their eyes,
The Lord restoring Lady Zion.
—Isaiah 52:8

Come to the Water

All you who are thirsty,
come to the water!
—Isaiah 55:1

Lonely Road

I run in the path of your commands,
for you have set my heart free.
—Psalm 119:32

Raised Up

"This is why I have raised you up, to show my
power through you that my name may be proclaimed
throughout the earth."
- Romans 9:17

The pelicans lined up in a perfect row as I approached on my paddleboard. It was as if they were standing up to watch me pass, viewing the Lords progress restoring me. Together, we had subdued the earth and all moving creatures.

Ascend

"Shake off the dust, ascend to the throne, Jerusalem."
—Isaiah 52:2

Lighthouse

Even the darkness will not be dark to you, the night will shine like the day, for darkness is as light to you.
—Psalm 139:12

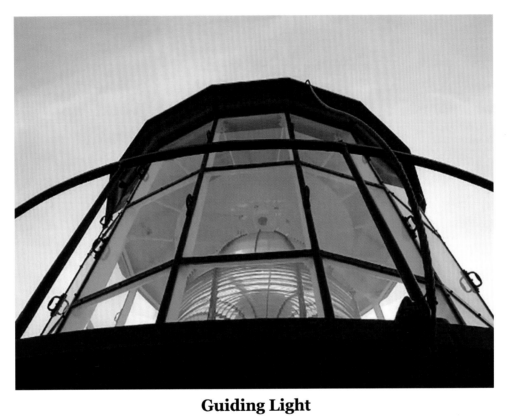

Guiding Light

For you were once darkness, but now you are light in the Lord
- Ephesians 5:8

2 Tribal Chant

The Lord refines me; the Spirit flows through me; sin is stripped.
The task presents itself as insurmountable, operating with Heaven's saints.
I can't quite grasp all the needed information while blindfolded and held in chains.
The Lord refines me; the Spirit flows through me; sin is stripped.

Stuck in a trance.

My flaws are presented; my weakness enhanced while
The Lord refines me; the Spirit flows through me; sin is stripped.
The information was there; I can't find it; my memory is wiped?
The Lord refines me; the Spirit flows through me; sin is stripped.

stuck in a trance.

Awake in a stupor.

I circle the funnel, and as the wind gradually slows,
The Lord refines me; the Spirit flows through me; sin is stripped.

Awake in a stupor.

The pieces fit; seven dimensions must converge;
The truth of my existence, beginning to emerge.
The Lord refines me; the Spirit flows through me; sin is stripped.

Stagger to find footing.

The image is distasteful, but onward I trudge.
My temple highjacked by evil spirits;

stagger to find footing.

The Lord refines me; the Spirit flows through me; sin is stripped.
Now a slave to their greed and self-fulfilling endeavors.

Stagger to find footing.

The Lord refines me; the Spirit flows through me; sin is stripped.
Too many years lost, digging to climb out   from a life lived underground.
The Lord refines me; the Spirit flows through me; sin is stripped.
Have they captured the correct person? Could they really need me?

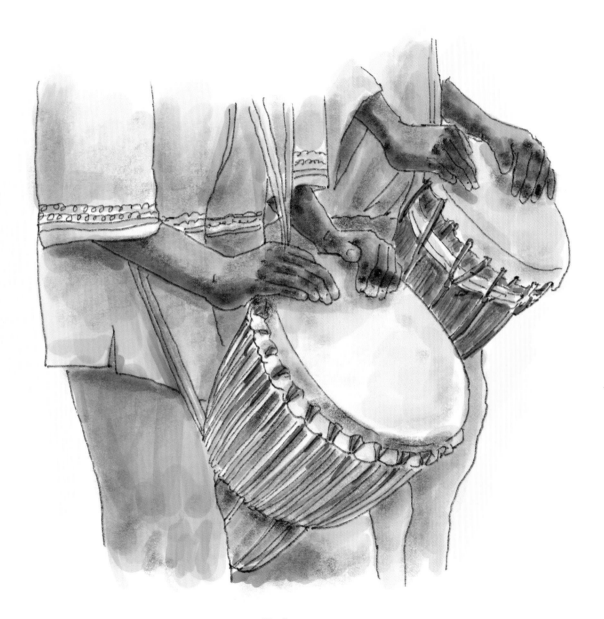

Tribal Beat

Exhausted by the journey, between these dimensions,
Pulling double duty, trying to meet expectations.
The Lord refines me; the Spirit flows through me; sin is stripped.

God's word now inside me, I AM   infused with new life.
The Lord refines me; the Spirit flows through me; sin is stripped.
Surrounded by God's Army—I AM   infused with new life.
The Lord refines me; the Spirit flows through me; sin is stripped.

The Lord refines me; the Spirit flows through me; sin is stripped,
I elevate out of earthly stupor, my eyes focus, and my ears tune in.
The Lord refines me; the Spirit flows through me; sin is stripped,
A primitive tribal chant echoes in my mind, my heart races, my temple rotates;
I understand the words they are chanting—

                                                              infused with new life.

                                                              Now I stand up.

"King David, King David, King David ..."
"Virgin Bride, Virgin Bride, Virgin Bride ..."

*And we bring you the good news, that what God promised to the father, this he has
fulfilled to us their children by raising Jesus; as also it is written in the second psalm,
"You are my Son, today I have begotten you. And as for the fact that he raised him from
the dead, no more to return to corruption, he spoke in this way, I will give you the holy
and sure blessing of David. Therefore, he says also in another psalm, you will not let
your Holy One see corruption. For David, after he had served the counsel of God in his
own generation, fell asleep and was laid with his fathers, and saw corruption; but he
whom God raised up saw no corruption. Let it be known to you therefore, brethren, that
through this man forgiveness of sin is proclaimed to you, and by him every one that believes is freed from everything from which you could not be freed by the law of Moses."*
—Acts 13:32-39

Standing Up

3 Glorious Heights

I notice in my travels that there is chaos overhead.
As I enter   and   exit buildings,
_____   work is happening above.   _____
                                                                    up,
                                                         running
                                               hoses

Ceiling tiles missing with

Babble Knot

while wires hang

d
  o
w
  n.

Fixtures being installed, and bulbs replaced,
from a leaking roof covering wires
that used to shed light.

Pipes and cables exposed overhead at Airport Concourse B
leaves me curious to know what's above I should see.
As I drive down the road, homes are under repair:
siding replaced, downspouts emptied, and windows cleaned.
Was there a sale on ladders I missed?
Why so much happening up above?
Was looking up expanding my temple, to glorious ancient heights?
Heights don't scare me—I have climbed a time or two.

I climbed a tree to collect mulberries when I was just a kid
  —lowered a full bucket to my friends waiting on the ground.
Bombed my dad from the garage roof with a water balloon
  —just to get a laugh.
Visited Cedar Point and rode to the peaks of roller coasters
  —for the thrill of the fall.
Lived on the twenty-first floor of a tower in college and
  —was swayed by the wind.
Climbed a couple mountains with three little boys in tow
  —we made gravy at the top and watched it trickle down.
Rode an elevator to the top of a skyscraper or two
  —for the view of a big city.
Circled the stairs of a lighthouse and
  —peered out from the light.

Love's Heights

The view from the Vatican dome was a dazzling sight, while
Machu Picchu's ancient ruins furnished a rare panorama.
My flight to Heaven is at the top of my mind. I just landed on Earth and am trying to

u
  n
w
  i
n
  d.

Enlarge
the space for your tent,
spread out your tent cloths unsparingly; lengthen your ropes
and make firm your pegs. For you shall spread abroad to the right and
left; your descendants shall dispossess the nations and shall people the deserted cities.
—Isaiah 54:2–3

4 My Delight

Out of Reach

Delight

Halfway between Heaven and earth is where I'm in my perfect light;
Just you and me soaring one level out of sight;
Floating just above the surface is where I want to be.
You and me passing, where no one else can see;
You, my perfect lover, and I, your soon delight.
We soar above the earth, transcending time and space;
riding just above the surface—the perfect hiding place.
For you, my perfect lover, and me your ever delight.
It's a place no one can touch us, where you woo me with new sight.
Such joy you've planned out for us when we reach our glorious height.

Even though I felt the world had decided to write me off, my Father in Heaven most certainly had not; He had sent me Jesus, and we were having an extraordinary love affair just outside the reach of the world.

For Zion's sake, I will not be silent, for Jerusalem's sake I will not be quiet until her vindication shines forth like the dawn and her victory like a burning torch. Nations shall behold your vindication, and all kings your glory; You shall be called by a new name pronounced by the mouth of the Lord. You shall be a glorious crown in the hand of the Lord, a royal Diadem held by your God. No more shall men call you forsaken, or your land Desolate, but you shall be my Delight, and your land Espoused. For the Lord delights in you and makes your land his spouse. As a young man marries a virgin, your Builder shall marry you; And as a bridegroom rejoices in his bride so shall your God rejoice in you.
—Isaiah 62:1–5

5 Perfect Vision

Perfection

Having eyes to SEE Heaven continuously would be a beautiful thing. People often talk about "God spots" or Divine moments, but my vision of Heaven far exceeds a moment here and there. What started as Divine moments of seeing has grown exponentially over my years of seeking a relationship with Jesus. After a decade of seeking, Jesus revealed to me in a vision that I was now on a "fast track" to a union with him. This journey would require me to be exiled from the world and tethered to Jesus for seven years, ending in the perfect vision of Heaven and Earth.

     In the upper room of my mind one day, I asked Jesus when this union would happen, and he indicated that it would happen on May 7, but he did not give me a year. Several things became crystal-clear to me. First, the "fast track" in heaven is not at all fast on earth—at least in my opinion. It has been years since Jesus told me I was on the "fast track" in 2013. The number of completions in the Bible is seven, making 2020 the end of my exile, and fittingly, the beginning of perfect vision, progressing from empty human eyes to all-seeing eyes:

Perfect Vision—20/20

Second, I have been spinning in a tornado while being refined as sin is stripped away, leaving much information out of my view. How can I keep the scraps of information I collect as I spin in circles to piece together later?

On top of that, there are evil spirits in the "heavens" trying to derail me, which requires me to test the souls I encounter to confirm I gather accurate information. Multiple confirmations of where the data is coming from are needed to make Heaven and earth collide someday.

Will this complicated puzzle ever be finished?

Is it even possible?

And why has my life become a puzzle?

Finally, I am starting to lose interest in the human dimension; the polarity of my life moving from seeing Heaven to viewing earth is wearing me down. Heaven is my likely choice if I am required to reside in only one place, but my worry for my sons will not let me rest. I am a mother and unable to regress when it comes to the safety and wellbeing of my children.

On the bright side, my ability to be in Heaven and on earth in tandem has grown. It was the summer of 2016, year three of my "fast track" journey, and the refining tornado cycle was starting again. Heavenly spirits were working in a new way by stepping right through people to talk to me. Or maybe I was more tuned into the spiritual dimension and able to perceive their messages. The moments of my life that were "God spots" were becoming continuous.

While I was sitting out back one afternoon in the outdoor room with my husband Charles, suddenly Saint Joseph was talking to me directly through Charles' mouth. It was as if Charles faded into the background of his being, and Saint Joseph was using Charles' body, physical movements, and words to converse with me. I wish I could explain the power of the occurrence accurately, but I was talking to Charles and Saint Joseph in tandem. I could understand and keep up with both conversations, which was astonishing. Saint Joseph was telling me that I was his daughter, that he loved me, and had been wanting to come to me for some time now. I knew that I was Saint Joseph's daughter from previous dreams and visions, and now I was literally in his presence, conversing with him.

Charles's body and mouth asked me if I wanted to go to Waxhaw to get an ice cream cone. But for me it was Saint Joseph, in Heaven, taking me, his daughter, out for ice cream. I was so excited. We got our cones and sat outside on the bench in front of the parlor together. After we finished, Saint Joseph looked right through Charles at me and said, "I enjoyed our time together." My heart melted inside as I felt the Spirit course through my body with an electrifying tingling sensation, confirming that I was operating in the Spiritual dimension. Suddenly I felt safe, revitalized, and not at all lonely. When we finished our ice cream, Saint Joseph vanished, and Charles returned to the forefront of his being.

The next day, a similar thing occurred, except even better. Charles and I traveled out to Raleigh for work and to see our son, Jeffrey, at college. We had expanded our business to Raleigh and traveled there every couple of weeks. When we arrived, we picked Jeffrey up for dinner at his "hellhole," as I like to call it. Ten college boys living in one house was the equivalent of a hellhole no matter how you sliced or diced it. I always texted Jeffrey when I arrived and waited outside for him. Going inside would make me question leaving my son there. Because Jeffrey was in his twenties, I decided not even to let my mind struggle with the dilemma; clearly, I could not take him home with me, so why view his living conditions?

What happened that night at dinner was magnificent. Not only was I having dinner with Saint Joseph, who was talking to me directly through Charles, but I was also having dinner with Jesus, who was talking to me through Jeffrey. I was stunned. Mind you, Charles and Jeffrey had a conversation going on, but I could not focus on what they were saying because I was laser-focused on being in the presence of Jesus. Jesus looking right at me through Jeffrey's big beautiful brown eyes, and speaking to me with that sweet voice wholly enchanted me.

The most potent confirmation of Jesus's presence that night was when Jeffrey got out of the car after dinner. He said, "It was a pleasure having dinner with you two. Drive safely." I will never forget that moment as long as I live. Those were not at all words Jeffrey would ever use to say goodbye to us. He may have said, "Bye, Mom and Dad, love you." Or "Thanks for dinner, Mom and Dad. Love you guys." But the words I heard—"It was a pleasure having dinner with you two. Drive safely"—were definitive confirmation that I had just finished dinner with Jesus Christ.

The Voice of God in a Great Storm:

A Psalm of David

Ascribe to the Lord O heavenly beings, ascribe to the Lord glory and strength. Ascribe to the Lord the glory of his name; worship the Lord in holy splendor. The voice of the Lord is over the waters; the God of glory thunders, the Lord, over mighty waters. The voice of the Lord is powerful; the voice of the Lord is full of majesty. The voice of the Lord breaks the cedars; the Lord breaks the cedars of Lebanon. He makes Lebanon skip like a calf, and Sirion like a young wild ox. The voice of the Lord flashes forth flames of fire. The voice of the Lord shakes the wilderness; the Lord shakes the wilderness of Kadesh. The voice of the Lord causes the oaks to whirl, and strips the forest bare; and in his temple all say, "Glory!" The Lord sits enthroned over the flood; the Lord sits enthroned as king forever. May the Lord give strength to his people! May the Lord bless his people with peace!
—Psalm 29: 1-11

6 The Third Heaven

Third Heaven

Where is the Third Heaven? It's where I would prefer to be.
>   The heavens with evil spirits, leave thorns in my side.
I have asked many Christians, but can't seem to find
>   one who sees what I SEE or hides where I HIDE!
My love affair with Jesus is truly unique;
>   he finds me in dreams and holds me in chains.
I moved from one Queen city to another, where I currently reside. Held in a spiritual
>   dimension, as a prisoner of Christ.
A temple is being built, right in my head; I am repeatedly pruned back, in hopes of
>   reaching new heights.
Constructing a tall house, to enter someday, so I can speak God's word and
>   proclaim Her Holy name.
The veil lifted, revelation freely flows,
>   disclosing knowledge entirely unknown.
I headed to an outdoor concert, while in the third Heaven one evening.
>   The music was pure, as they sang right to me.
My eyes opened wide as I floated on cloud nine
>   until I stepped on broken glass in the gravel parking lot.
Blood poured out of my foot, and stitches were needed;
>   My suffering resumed; once again, I'm pruned.
"I would walk on broken glass to see Jesus once more."
>   Why I wrote that in my journal—I must have been bored.
Now more careful what I say, because it often happens the next day,
>   As heaven refines me to be Whole once again.

Shackles

I must boast; not that it is profitable, but I will go on to visions and revelations of the Lord. I know someone in Christ who, fourteen years ago (whether in the body or out of the body I do not know, God knows), was caught up to the third Heaven. And I know that this person (whether in the body or out of the body I do not know, God knows) was caught up into Paradise and heard ineffable things which no one may utter. About this person I will boast, but about myself I will not boast, except about my weaknesses. Although if I should boast, I would not be foolish, for I would be telling the truth. But I refrain, so that no one may think more of me than what he sees in me or hears from me because of the abundance of revelations. Therefore, I might not become too elated a thorn in the flesh was given to me, an angel of Satan to beat me, to keep me from being too elated. Three times I begged the Lord about this, that it might leave me, but he said to me, "My grace is sufficient for you, for power is made perfect in weakness." I will rather boast most gladly of my weakness, in order that the power of Christ dwell in me. Therefore, I am content with weaknesses, insults, hardships, persecutions and constraints for the sake of Christ.

For when I am weak,

I am strong.

—2 Corinthians 12:1-10

Crown of Thorns

7 Forever Green

For the gate is narrow and the road is hard that leads to life,
and there are few who find it.
—Matthew 7:14

I sat in the hospital emergency room waiting to get my foot stitched up after stepping on broken glass. While waiting, I remembered a previous trip to the ER a few years earlier. I don't recall precisely why I was there, other than the memory that heaven was flowing through me, and I couldn't stand on my own two feet looking like a sane person—I was bowled right over.

What I do recollect is staring at the television above me as the spirit was flowing powerfully through me. There was a documentary about Princess Diana on the TV. The commentator was discussing how Princess Diana married a man too old and mature for her; she had not yet "come into her own." The commentator concluded that Princess Diana was a free spirit, and Prince Charles was too old, restrained, and refined for her. Prince Charles was holding Princess Diana back, and the two were not a good match.

As I sat in the hospital room and watched the documentary, I heard a voice in my head say, "If I have to go get Buck to fix you, I will." I came unglued. What? Get my high school and college boyfriend to heal me! That's insane. I had not seen Buck for decades. Don't bother anyone to fix me. I don't want to disturb anybody's life to enable my repair—please leave Buck alone. I don't remember much else about that trip to the ER, but the threat of God going to get Buck to heal my soul would linger in my mind for years. I had a fear of making waves and facing pain, rejection, and heartache that I had no desire to face—not ever.

After that trip to the emergency room, I started questioning myself and the path I had taken in life: Had I not come into my own when I married my husband, Charles? Am I like Princess Diana, being in a relationship for which I am not well suited? Could my whole life be a farce? Am I just getting by and not feeling? My husband is a little more than seven years older than me, and without question, more restrained and polished. Maybe am I too "green" to be married

19

to someone as spiritually beautiful and refined as Charles? I am certainly more of a free spirit and a rule-breaker, while Charles is upstanding, refined, and dutiful. The comparison made sense, but it was more than I could digest. Me, broken, not whole, and God coming to fix me. Bothering people who were busy trying to live their lives to do so. Potentially making Charles, the most beautiful Spirit I knew, sad or mad. And bothering Buck, who was likely living a beautiful life—this was unacceptable.

I did not want to rock the boat.

I did not want to hurt anyone.

I can suck it up.

I will endure.

Why did it take me so long to contemplate my life choices and the path I was on?

Had I rushed through life, not taking time to decide where I was headed and why?

Path Travailed

8 Rescattered

And I looked, and behold a white cloud, and upon the cloud one sat like unto the Son of man, having on his head a golden crown, and in his hand a sharp sickle.
—Revelation 14:14

Harvest

My youngest son, Nicholas, decided to hop a fence one day because he didn't have a key for the gate. Now Nicholas is very agile, athletic, and fearless, but this fence was high, and he missed. Just barely, but he missed. The metal point at the top of the fence went right through his forearm, and blood started to pour out. Charles and I met Nicholas at the ER, where he arrived by ambulance, and the doctors determined that he would need stitches and possibly surgery. Nick literally had a hole in his arm that had to be stitched up. Nerves were severed, and he lost feeling on the back of his hand. Subsequent surgery did not repair the loss of sensation.

Nicholas was no stranger to the ER. We had taken him to the hospital many times over the years. The trauma started when he was two, when the corner of a booth at the Tiger Deli met the side of his head, adding seven threaded stitches to his scalp as well as a spot where no hair can grow. A baseball connected with the back of Nick's scalp when he agreed to hang out behind the bounce-back while his brother was practicing pitching. This resulted in nine staples being gunned into the back of his head and another scar where no hair can grow. Once a mailbox jumped out into the middle of the road as Nicholas was biking down the street. He did a full front tuck in the air before cracking his chest smack dab on top of the metal mailbox and then bounced back, landing on the sidewalk. The doozy up until the failed fence hop was Nick's first run at the skateboard park in full protective gear. He broke his arm, and I could see the bone protruding out of his flesh. That accident required morphine for Nicholas, and a nurse had me sit with my head between my knees so I wouldn't pass out. His brothers' favorite story is when Nicholas was goofing around and decided to stab himself with what he thought was my practice EpiPen cartridge; it turned out to be the real injector, loading Nick with an unneeded dose of adrenaline. According to his older brothers, the look on Nick's face was priceless. I wasn't home for that one, and his father had to deal with the ER trip and manage the tormenting by his older brothers.

While waiting for Nicholas to get stitches from the failed fence hop, my mind deliberated: Why his arm? My thoughts moved back in time a few years to when God filled my mind with massive amounts of information about Biblical history. God explained that Benjamin and Jeffrey had unique spiritual gifts that were given to them long ago. Then, when God was explaining to me how he was rescattering his people, Nick was moved to a different group in the process due to sins. My sins or familial sins, I wasn't sure, but I cried for hours at the time of this revelation. As I looked at the picture of Nicholas and me from when he was a baby, I wondered if maybe he could have been an arm of god—one made to suffer for the cross. Did I hurt Nicholas or help him due to my sins or familial sins? I was not entirely sure, but if I had any say in it, I would have taken whatever punishment was necessary to make sure Nicholas never suffered.

As I sat there watching Nicholas grimace in pain while his arm was stitched up, my heart ached for him and ached to remember how I felt that day hearing he would be rescattered somewhere separate from his brothers. I couldn't imagine a God who would separate his or her children. It didn't make sense. If I am the one holding the sickle, I will cut anyone down who tries to separate my children. It won't happen. Anyone who messes with my children has messed with the wrong Mother.

As my mind rolled through the memory, tears began to trickle down my cheeks. I've always had a difficult time expressing my feelings, but they are in there. One thing I can assure you: I will not let Nicholas suffer or be denied anything because of something I did. I will figure out how to fix this and keep my children together.

Wield the sickle,
for the harvest is ripe;
Come and tread,
for the wine press is full;
The vats overflow,
for their crimes are numerous.
Crowds upon crowds
in the Valley of Decision;
For near is the day of the Lord in the Valley of Decision.
Sun and moon are darkened,
and the stars withhold their brightness,
The Lord roars from Zion,
and from Jerusalem raises his voice,
The heavens and the earth quake,
but the Lord will be a shelter for his people,
a fortress for the people of Israel.

Sickle

A Secure Future for Judah

Then you will know that I am the Lord your God,
*   dwelling on Zion, my Holy mountain;*
Jerusalem will be Holy,
*   and strangers will never again travel through her.*
On that day
*   the mountains will drip new wine,*
*   and the hills flow with milk,*
All the streams of Judah
*   will flow with water.*
A spring will rise from the house of the Lord ,
*   watering the Valley of Shittim.*
Egypt will be a waste,
*   Edom a desolate wilderness,*
Because of violence done to the Judahites,
*   because they shed innocent blood in their land.*
But Judah will be inhabited forever,
*   and Jerusalem for all generations.*
I will avenge their blood,
*   and I will not acquit the guilt.*
*   The Lord dwells in Zion.*
—Joel 4: 13-21

Waterfall

9 Future Glory

I have been crucified with Christ; it is no longer I who live, but Christ who lives in me; and the life I now live in the flesh I live by faith in the Son of God, who loved me and gave himself for me.
—Galatians 2:19–20

It was 2016, and my husband Charles and I, now empty nesters, decided to do some traveling. I liked to keep busy and find places to uncover Heaven by visiting religious and historic buildings and sites. I wanted to live in the present and live fully, not plan for a future my life may never discover. I was tired of saving for later and planning for a retirement that I may not be alive to enjoy. My mom died in her mid-forties and my dad in his early fifties. They didn't get to travel to the places they wanted to see, enjoy retirement, or meet their grandchildren. I was determined not to make the same mistakes. I was going to live within my means but chase my dreams. I had a go-big or go-home attitude, a midlife crisis, or maybe both.

Charles and I ventured to Spain and Italy with his sister and her family. It was nice to interact and travel with other people; we didn't do that often. I was accustomed to functioning daily while feeling Jesus's suffering. I had been enduring the pain for several years now, and the severity waxed and waned throughout my journey. The episodes had grown in frequency and magnitude in recent years. While family members were aware of what I was experiencing, they never brought it up. I'm not sure why.

We enjoyed a few days in Spain visiting our niece and her husband. Italy was our next stop and my favorite place to travel. A place to collect pieces of the puzzle I was putting together about Heaven, as well as the meaning of Biblical Scripture and history. I have a keen eye for seeing through Scripture and art, and for hearing Heaven's truths via gifts of the Holy Spirit. For example, I would look at a piece of artwork, and a Scripture I read the day before would pop into my head. And then the next day, I would be looking at a photo album, and I would see a picture that reminded me of the artwork at the Vatican. Or I would snap a photo, and the light would yield a flash that looked like a sickle in my hand on the same day that I read a passage about a sickle and noticed a new scar on my wrist in the same shape. Three confirmations of the same message told me that my intuition about revelation was accurate. Sometimes it would take years to get those confirmations, and other times, they would come all at once.

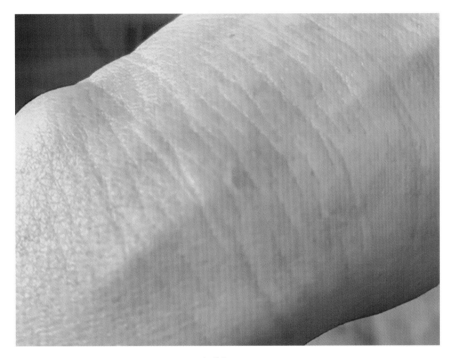

Sickle Scar

Divine truths not written in history or theology books were being revealed to me. I gained a mystical understanding of Heaven by collecting bits and pieces of information here and there over time, gleaning accurate conclusions. I was Sherlock Holmes in disguise—a great disguise as the mother of three sons in her early fifties, not a likely sleuth out discovering mysteries about the unknown universal present as well as secrets of the ancient past.

In Rome, we toured the Vatican, where I located the Delphic Sybil, a new curiosity of mine and a piece of the puzzle given to me from Heaven. I saw a picture of the Delphic Sybil a few years back and was intrigued. As I researched her, I started having dreams and visions about her role in history; she was the most powerful prophetess and Goddess from ancient times. I became convinced that I was connected to her somehow or meant to uncover something about her.

The history of the Delphic Sybil made me think of an expression Papa used to say to me when I was a young girl: "Glad to see you back from the front, old top." Papa would pat my back, then pat my belly, and then tap me on the head as he recited his silly saying. Now I imagine that maybe Papa was right: I am the Delphic Sybil at the front lines of this insane cosmic war, and my head is the old top—

Anyway, before reaching the Sistine Chapel, we strolled down the Gold Hall where a painting caught my eye. The Holy Spirit indicated through a voice inside my ear, or a locution, that said the image was a message intended for me. "Look," it said, followed by a tingling sensation that coursed through my body, giving me the chills of understanding that the Spirit frequently offers. I examined the details of the painting and the woman carrying a crucifix. It crossed my mind that **the Holy Spirit from Heaven would one day be poured out like that on me.**

The separation between Heaven and Earth in the painting reminded me of how I viewed Charlotte, North Carolina, a few years back. I saw the sky separated from the ground by a layer of clouds as the Holy Spirit flowed through me. The weather was unusual that day, moving from sunny and bright to windy and overcast, quickly and unnaturally; weather shifts unlike anything I had ever witnessed. The best description would be a thick layer of clouds settling directly between the concrete and the city, leaving my feet on the ground and my head above the clouds.

The clay pot being crushed on earth in the artwork made me think of the cluster of blood vessels knotted in my brain that was discovered back in 1999 when I contracted a neurologic virus. Revelation through Scripture made it clear that I was a vessel made empty for the heavens' use. The illness, however, left me experiencing far less than my full abilities. My mind was crushed. I experienced numbness on the right side of my body, floaters in my vision, pain in my spinal cord and neck, and, most notably, years of my life when I was unable to express myself fully or access God's temple in my head. The only thing I gained was a routine life, going through the motions. My existence was one of far less enthusiasm than one enjoys when living wholly.

Golden Hall

The ladies painting the woman being glorified are saints, ministering to the blessed woman from Heaven and painting her in bright colors. I became hopeful when I saw the painting that the woman may be a view of my future after my restoration.

What looks like a camera below the clouds makes me think of the spinning sensation frequently circling my head like a halo, the physical movement in the direction of a Rolodex turning on its side like a cinematic film, either recording or playing something back.

To gain knowledge and vision where one resides free of earthly constraints, a peace not seen by most today.

This is the pact that I made with you when you came out of Egypt, and my Spirit continues in your midst: Do not fear! For thus says the Lord of hosts: One moment yet, a little while, and I will shake the heavens and the earth, the sea and the dry land. I will shake all the nations, and the treasures of all the nations will come in, and I will fill this house with glory, says the Lord of hosts. Mine is the silver and Mine the gold, says the Lord of hosts. Greater will be the future glory of this house than the former, says the Lord of hosts: And in this place I will give peace, says the Lord of hosts!
—Haggai 2:5–9

10 A View from Above

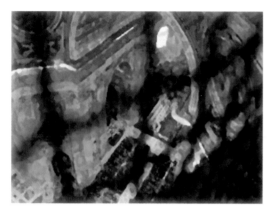

A View From Above

Narrow Passage

My View

Isolated from the world with a view from above.
Circling the dome
    —exploring expanses unknown.

Caged off from humanity, the view is obscure. Floating
in the heavens
    —the life of a drone.

God's movement now approaching—people kaleido-
scope away. Fragmenting into
    —translucent particles in space.

Each grain of sand, molecule, raindrop, and fingerprint,
the movement of God
    —my focus hones in.

Detached from my body, floating in the depths, my
desire to escape
    —momentarily fades away.

Human form constrains me from blending right in, I
land back on earth to look up and
    —ponder the magnificence of the master plan.

No words that I know can describe the feeling of transcending ones body, time, and space, to view the world from above. Once past the feeling of terror due to not understanding what is happening, the experience is quite magnificent—a granular look at how everything pieces together, and where each item belongs in order to complete everything to perfection. I imagine the feeling of enlightment might be the way Newton felt when he discovered gravity or the way Edison felt when he was successful inventing the lightbulb. I had a feeling of satisfaction in understanding, while at the same time, felt overwhelmed that it was me grasping such mysteries.

On many occasions, I prayed for the adrenalin rush that went along with each flight, but after one occasion where I felt like I might not ever reconnect with my human body again, I prayed to never take flight again. That prayer would not be answered. I was an empty vessel being used, and I had no ability to stop or deter my destiny.

The Good Shepherd

"Amen, amen, I say to you, whoever does not enter a sheepfold through the gate but climbs over elsewhere is a thief and a robber. But whoever enters through the gate is the shepherd of the sheep. The gatekeeper opens it for him, and the sheep hear his voice, as he calls his own sheep by name and leads them out. When he has driven out all his own, he walks ahead of them, and the sheep follow him, because they recognize his voice. But they will not follow a stranger; they will run away from him, because they do not recognize the voice of strangers." Although Jesus used this figure of speech, they did not realize what he was trying to tell them.
—John 10: 1-6

11 A Priestess

Chalice

And you and your sons with you shall attend to your priesthood for all that concerns the altar and that is within the veil; and you shall serve. I give your priesthood as a gift, and anyone else who comes near shall be put to death.
—Numbers 18:7

Enslaved

The priests want something—information garnered from above.
Their sermons demand prophets disclose what they've unearthed,
Because gifts of the Spirit are meant to be shared!
The pressure is immense—an omnidirectional attack,
              To drop my dreams and pick up those of Jesus.

I have needed information; why don't I speak?
They expect Heavenly fruit to be dropped at their feet!
While Jesus is telling me, it's not time to speak!
I'm obedient and hold wisdom till it's time,
              When Heaven opens fully, revealing knowledge from the vine.

Earthly authorities strike me with crushing accusations;
"It's not about you—it's about the greater good!"
The load now unbearable; an intrusive violation;
Heaven saying one thing while the world proclaims another.
              Wisdom will be revealed when the stars are aligned.

The timing's not mine—I am enslaved,
by unschooled powers, demanding I cave;
God cares about my dreams, and will make them come true,
If the heavens don't understand that, I'll happily tell them what to do.
              Nobody will listen—I retreat deep within.

In time I relent to overwhelming pressure,
And ask Jesus to erase my dreams, and instead give me his!
His response reaffirmed his eternal devotion:
"Your dreams won't be dropped—instead I will make them mine;
              Our union now approaching; our dreams will happen in time!

Dream

Standing behind a massive, life-size chalice, I saw two long pointed hexagonal stones descending from Heaven toward the chalice. The stones disappeared into the sky, and the chalice turned into an altar. I stepped forward and was presiding at the banquet table.

I heard God call out, "Daughter." I answered, "Yes, Father?"

In Zion the Lord has made feast and Sabbath to be forgotten; He has scorned in fierce wrath both king and priest. The Lord has disowned his altar, rejected his sanctuary; the walls of her towers he has handed over to the enemy, who shout in the house of the Lord as on a feast day. The Lord marked for destruction the wall of daughter Zion: He stretched out the measuring line; his hand brought ruin, yet he did not relent—He brought grief on wall and rampart till both succumbed. Sunk into the ground are her gates; he has removed and broken her bars. Her king and her princes are among the pagans; priestly instruction is wanting, and her prophets have not received any vision from the Lord.
—Lamentations 2:6–9

Gate

12 Under My Roof

The Lord came down to see the city and the tower which the sons of men had built.
—Genesis 11:5

I could feel the construction going on in my brain as cubits were crunched into my head, stacking higher and higher, while blood vessels extended my vine to the east and the west, opening my mind to revelation and original thought. God's temple was being built in my head.

I was curious to know what the measurement of a cubit was, so I Googled it and found a definition that said it was the length from one's elbow to the tip of one's middle finger. I decided it was not a numerical measurement at all since everybody has different armlengths. I happen to have unusually long arms, so my temple would be larger than the average person my size. It seemed to me that the cubit had an entirely different meaning all together.

Anyway, something exquisite happened around the midpoint of my temple construction. I prayed to see Jesus again; it had been two years since I stood before Him. I was overshadowed one morning when Jesus showed up in Spirit. Jesus leaned his forehead against mine, nose to nose, and said, "Amy, my love, may I enter under your roof?" I melted instantly, overwhelmed that Jesus would ask permission to look at what he was building. Jesus has a way of softening me like no other. I said, "Yes, you can enter."

When he entered, my temple physically started to rotate like a halo; I could feel the pressure building in my head. I am not sure what Jesus was checking or where my temple was in the building process, but the thought of him inside me melted my heart and strengthened my soul. I was his beloved, and I longed for the day when I would become one with him.

Eternal Love

Mutual Delight in Each Other
"Where has your beloved gone,
O most beautiful among women?
Where has your beloved turned,
That we may seek him with you?"
My beloved has gone down to his garden,
To the beds of balsam,
To pasture his flock in the gardens
And gather lilies.
"I am my beloved's and my beloved is mine,
He who pastures his flock among the lilies."
You are as beautiful as Tirzah, my darling,
As lovely as Jerusalem,
As awesome as an army with banners.
"Turn your eyes away from me,
For they have confused me;
Your hair is like a flock of goats
That have descended from Gilead.
Your teeth are like a flock of ewes
Which have come up from their washing,
All of which bear twins,
And not one among them has lost her young.
Your temples are like a slice of a pomegranate
Behind your veil.
There are sixty queens and eighty concubines,
And maidens without number;
But my dove, my perfect one, is unique:
She is her mother's only daughter;
She is the pure child of the one who bore her.
The maidens saw her and called her blessed,

The queens and the concubines also, and they praised her, saying,
'Who is this that grows like the dawn,
As beautiful as the full moon,
As pure as the sun,
As awesome as an army with banners?'
I went down to the orchard of nut trees
To see the blossoms of the valley,
To see whether the vine had budded
Or the pomegranates had bloomed.
Before I was aware, my soul set me
Over the chariots of my noble people.
Come back, come back, O Shulammite;
Come back, come back, that we may gaze at you!
Why should you gaze at the Shulammite,
As at the dance of the two companies?
—Song of Songs 6:1-13

Eternal Love

13 The Upper Room

But when you pray, go to your inner room, close the door and pray to your
Father in secret.
—Matthew 6:6

Not long after our trip to Italy, something anomalous and authentic started happening to me during Mass. When I would kneel during the preparation of the banquet table on earth, I would close my eyes and spiritually transport to Heaven, where I was at the table with Jesus Christ, his disciples, angels, and saints. My body was on earth, but my mind spiritually escaped and resided in Heaven. The temple building was most definitely working; my mind could go places and do things that I had never experienced before or even dreamed.

I saw Heaven with my third eye blind or mind's eye. It's not the way one sees with human eyes but a "present Spiritual" view of Heaven. The best way I can describe it is this: Close your eyes and conjure a picture in your mind of the upper room and imagine you are at the banquet table. Suddenly, everything comes to life; you are no longer in control of the scene you imagined but interacting in a new reality, and Jesus is directing the scene. It is every bit as real as this world. Maybe even more authentic—a connection to the origin of existence, the first spark, the basal vibration. It's more beautiful than what is happening on earth. For me, this type of Spiritual "seeing" is far less startling than other types of "seeing" I have experienced in recent years when I have seen things people around me couldn't. The actual seeing with human eyes is effortless to grasp and hold onto, but far more startling.

Fascinatingly, time somehow stands still when I am in the upper room. What would be a twenty-minute conversation on earth between Jesus and me takes maybe three minutes in the upper chamber. I absorb what Jesus is telling me by merely being in his presence, as if by osmosis. The conversations that I have had with Jesus during communion are extensive. I am going to share a few experiences to give you a sense of how the interaction happens, along with a few key things I learned.

One of the first things that Jesus wanted me to understand was that I must keep my eyes fixed on him. If I was going to do his work here on earth, I could not listen to the priests, the government, or anybody else in my life to determine if what I hear in the heavens is accurate. Jesus was going to teach me what was right, and I needed to detach myself from the people and community I rely on and depend solely on him.

Sound simple? I assure you it is not. Think about how much you rely on the church, the government, your doctor, your spouse, a parent, a teacher, and maybe your best friend when making a decision—in other words, on people or institutions with a physical presence that can validate what you are thinking and feeling to provide feedback. I had to abandon my support system and operate independently to do what Jesus was asking. It's more distressing than I ever imagined, particularly when what Jesus was asking me to do was contrary to what's socially acceptable, indoctrinated by the church, or deemed legal by the government.

Jesus reminded me repeatedly for years to keep my eyes fixed on him. When the world was caving in around me, luring me in the wrong direction, or feeding me false information, he would direct me. During my refinement cycles, I collected pieces of information about myself through time and space, trying to pull the story of me together. The more homogenized I became, the easier it was to keep my eyes fixed on Jesus.

Open Door

Meditation

Jesus has been waiting patiently for my arrival. Over the years, he has whispered gently, calling me to him, and I have often thought to myself:

Am I hearing things?

How did that happen?

Was that a coincidence?

Now, having sought Jesus out during a time of need, and finally having heard him calling me, I respond:

I arrive at the door of the dimly lit upper room; looking in, I see Jesus standing in the shadows with his arm stretched out toward me. I grab hold of Jesus' hand, and we begin our journey together. I take a step toward Jesus. He pulls me toward him and into the room, the shadows now behind us. Standing in his presence, I am mesmerized by his gentle yet piercing eyes gazing down on me. Warmth spreads from my core and moves outward through every cell in my body, embracing me with a peaceful tingling sensation. Now relaxed, my heart feels settled and at home—the safety one feels sitting next to a warm fire protecting you from the elements of a developing blizzard outside. I am not entirely sure where I am or how I am, but I know I would like to stay forever.

Jesus, knowing that I am not quite sure what to do next, takes the lead and steps toward me. While still holding my left hand with his right hand, he places his left hand on my waist and draws me closer to him. He smiles gently at me and says, "Beloved, I have been waiting for you. I am so happy you are here; I love you. Please tell me everything in your heart; I want to hear it all."

14 Nonslip Mat

And not only this, but we also exult in God through our Lord Jesus Christ, through whom we have now received the reconciliation.
—Romans 5:11

By early March 2017, experiences in the upper room of my mind during Mass intensified. I was hearing and understanding Heaven and earth in unison. One day during the elementary school Mass at my parish, the children were singing with timid voices. I was disheartened to see children so shy about vocalizing joy; I was straining to hear their words. Then, when the next verse of the song started, I could hear the children in Heaven singing in tandem with the children on Earth. It was refreshing to hear children living fully, shouting pure joy out to the universe with passion. Heaven on Earth sounds far more appealing than earth without Heaven. If I can see Heaven on Earth daily, then my desire to stay on this planet may be rekindled.

Soon after this transpired, my daily experiences in the upper room of my mind during Mass shifted to the sacrament of reconciliation. I was sitting with Jesus and confessing my sins. I had been confessing my sins to Jesus for years now, but something was different. During the "wash-and-spin cycle" I endured, sins that resided in the darkest corners of my soul sprang forth, and I was forced to face my life head-on. I had no choice but to comply. What was different now was that I was sitting in Jesus' presence in the upper room of my mind, where we were talking openly about everything like friends would.

My confession to Jesus went on for several days: at Mass in the upper room of my mind, in dreams, and even in visions. As I went through my day, I would surprisingly be reminded of something else I needed to tell Jesus about. I sensed the angels and saints were hovering around, poking and prodding me, saying, "Amy, don't forget to tell Him" this or that. I was continually made aware of everything I had done wrong in my lifetime. The angels, saints, and spirits in the heavens shook me up, tossed me around, and squeezed out as much sin as they could.

When I was sitting with Jesus sharing my mistakes, I was being caressed by the perfect lover; somehow, he gently exposed my flaws without making me feel bad. Instead, I felt his love being poured out to me as if he was sad that I had to endure the world and commit my sins at all. Jesus forgave me immediately, and my shame instantly vanished. If Jesus forgave me, then why would I possibly care how anyone else might judge me? Jesus told me that I was worthy of union with him because he made me that way. For all the worrying I had done, Jesus' forgiveness was instantaneous. I felt a weight lift off me and a freedom wash over me that I had not known since my youth.

The same day at Mass when I knelt after receiving communion, a line miraculously appeared before my eyes on my right hand—a physical sign confirming my reconciliation.

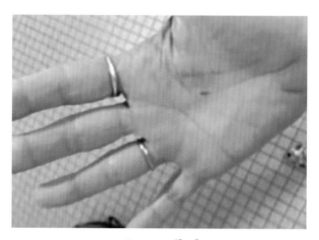

Reconciled

Being reconciled to Jesus was much better than any confession I had made to a priest on earth. Being a convert, and clearly not a good Catholic, I had not gone to confession more than a handful of times over the years. I dialed up the big guy myself and told Jesus what was on my mind directly. Confessing to a priest always felt awkward.

I understand going to the person that you have offended or wronged, telling them what you did, and saying you were sorry. That's what my mom made us do growing up. I find that harder than telling an unaffected third party.

I didn't do too many things that were wrong as a child. Once I stole a miniature plastic Barbie McDonald's hamburger from my neighbor, Wendy, and my mom marched me over to Wendy's front door and made me tell her and her mom what I had done and that I was sorry. I did feel better afterward. We played Barbies daily together for months after that. Confessing to the person I offend lifts the weight and pressure, allowing the relationship to advance with a full breath.

A Dream

Not long after my reconciliation with Jesus, I had a lucid dream where I was taking a bath, and Jesus was sitting next to me, talking to me while I bathed. After I finished, Jesus picked the nonslip bathmat up out of the tub and tucked it under his arm. He held out his other hand, I grabbed hold tightly, and we continued our journey. It was as if I was covered for life now—all my sins washed away before I even committed them. And Jesus and I both knew that I would. Being reconciled to Jesus was the equivalent of having a nonslip mat. You can't fall anywhere without Jesus arriving and picking you up. I smiled at him as we continued down the path, and Jesus said to me, "Beloved, be sure to tell everybody that I have a nonslip bathmat for them too."

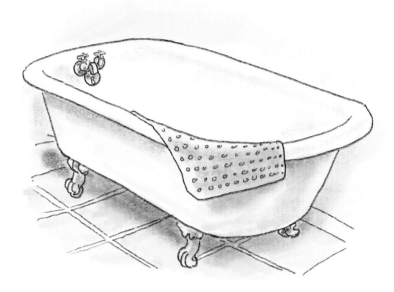

Nonslip Mat

15 Jesus Takes the Wheel

Flee from Babylon; escape with your lives! Do not be destroyed in her punishment. For this is the time of the Lord s vengeance; He will pay her what she deserves. Babylon was a gold cup in the hand of the Lord making the whole earth drunk. The nations drank her wine; therefore, the nations have gone mad. Suddenly Babylon has fallen and been shattered. Wail for her; get her balm for her pain; perhaps she can be healed.
—Jeremiah 51:6–8

Jesus handed me a chalice at the banquet table in the upper room of my mind one day;

It was gold and studded with shimmering stones.

I thought it a blessing until I realized it meant suffering.

The Lord overshadowed me and was operating my body—

I was no longer in control, Jesus now at the wheel!

Present in multiple dimensions while able to move forward,

I was viewing my body's actions but no longer controlling my movements.

Where would we go, and what would we say? I didn't know,

But I surrendered and relinquished control.

Jesus remotely steered as we drove to Mass one warm spring morning;

We parked in the church parking lot, got out, and locked the car doors.

And as we walked up the path to the church, I heard Jesus's footsteps,

Loud and deliberate—he was walking right next to me!

I took a deep breath, not knowing what to expect.

My head now held high; I took each step with extraordinary confidence,

Entering the doors of the church to find the priest in the narthex.

My mouth opened, but the words that came out were not mine.

Jesus asked Father Bill for assistance in presiding over Mass

As if I would be standing at the altar on earth.

Father Bill declared me a heretic: "No woman will ever be a priest!"

Jesus spoke right through me and assured Father Bill he was wrong.

In the next instant, I realized I was in control of my own body again

because suddenly, I was uncertain of the declaration just made.

Without Jesus present, I became far less resolute.

Would the Heavenly occurrences in my mind start happening on earth?

Could I stand at the altar and preach God's message?

Bless Heaven's gifts and serve at the banquet table?

I closed my eyes to pray for courage and

saw two clear images in my eyelids.

The first was a cross with nobody on it, but I was standing at the base.

The second image had six lights shining on the ground and

The cross in the background engulfed in flames.

**At that moment, I realized Christ was rising in me—
I was the arm, now in motion, extending God's hand down to earth.**

Burning Cross

When the feast was already half over, Jesus went up into the temple area and began to teach. The Jews were amazed and said, "How does he know Scripture without having studied?" Jesus answered them and said, my teaching is not my own but is from the one who sent me. Whoever chooses to do his will shall know whether my teaching is from God or whether I speak on my own. Whoever speaks on his own seeks his own glory, but whoever seeks the glory of the one who sent him is truthful, and there is no wrong in him.
—John 7:14–18

16 Under a Bushel

Jesus claimed me as his mouthpiece years ago through Scripture when he woke me in the middle of the night with a voice telling me out loud to read Acts of the Apostles 23:11, which indicated that I would proclaim his name to small and large crowds of people. And as God's mouthpiece, there would be no more hiding behind others.

I had faded into the background for years behind my husband:

- His captivating stories of how his parents met.

- His moving to Ireland and then escaping back to the US.

- His Wharton degree and career successes, leading to patents in his name.

I would defer attention to my boys:

- Their talent, success, infectious personalities, and handsome good looks.

I even had magnificent friends throughout my life:

- Friends who captured the attention of the crowds in which we socialized.

Not that it was anyone's fault but my own. I could have fought my way to the forefront, but I didn't; I simply had lost confidence. I got completely lost after my illness in 1999 and couldn't find my way back to the surface. As the arm and mouthpiece of God, I would now be forced to be somebody myself. The thought scared me and excited me at the same time:

To matter again ...

I couldn't see a clear path to completing the task God assigned me, given the constraints imposed: remaining in the Catholic Church while taking on a leadership role as a woman. One morning at Mass, Father Bill let me know that he was uncomfortable serving me communion because he believed I was a heretic. I had only told him what I understood through revelation: one day, very soon, women will be priests. But he didn't believe me so there didn't seem to be any point in arguing with him, at least not yet.

During the Gospel that day, Father Bill read this Scripture:

Jesus said to them, "If God were your Father, you would love me, for I came from God and am here; I did not come on my own, but he sent me."
—John 8:31–42

My entire body tingled …

I could feel Jesus present in me, coursing right through my veins. And when Father Bill stood up to start serving communion, I heard Jesus say, "Take a knee and leave the chapel now." So I did. Jesus had renewed me directly from the inside out so I could respect Father Bill's request to not receive communion at a table he presided over. A couple of weeks after that, Father Bill was promoted to a position uptown. With his exit from the parish, I could again partake at daily Mass while being obedient.

Disciples and the World

"You are the salt of the earth; but if the salt has become tasteless, how can it be made salty again? It is no longer good for anything, except to be thrown out and trampled under foot by men.

"You are the light of the world. A city set on a hill cannot be hidden; nor does anyone light a lamp and put it under a basket, but on the lampstand, and it gives light to all who are in the house. Let your light shine before men in such a way that they may see your good works and glorify your Father who is in heaven.
—Matthew 5:13–16

Under a Bushel

17 The Spirit Bears Witness

The Spirit Himself bears witness with our spirit that we are children of God, and if children, then heirs—heirs of God and joint heirs with Christ, if indeed we suffer with Him, that we may also be glorified together.
—Romans 8:16

I always seek three confirmations of everything I hear from the heavens. Evil spirits in the heavens are trying to derail me from following God's path. It's essential to continuously pray and seek a heavenly corroboration to reaffirm the revelation flowing into my mind.

A third confirmation that women were meant to be priestesses came not long after Father Bill was promoted and transferred to another parish. I was at morning Mass, and during the "Our Father," the Spirit was talking through me. I spoke the prayer like this: "Our Father who art in Heaven, hallowed be thy name. Thy Kingdom come, thy will be done, on earth as it is in heaven. Give us this day our daily bread and forgive us our trespasses as we forgive those who trespass against Him" … Instead of saying "trespass against us," I said, "trespass against Him." Was the Spirit telling me that I, a woman, would forgive people on behalf of Jesus Christ?

I asked Jesus daily if I could leave the Catholic Church and find another church where women had a leadership role. I didn't understand how I was going to accomplish Jesus's goals in the Catholic Church. But, leaving was nonnegotiable, and I was frustrated. It's not like I could sign up for admission to the seminary and become a priest. I am a woman, not a man—wrong body parts for a position of authority in the Catholic Church. I would likely scare the priests anyway; the revelation I hear from Heaven contradicts many practices of the Catholic Church, leaving me trapped between a rock and a hard place. I guess being squeezed is a part of my crusade through the wilderness. I keep my eyes fixed on Jesus, I'm obedient, and if Jesus Christ has a plan, why argue?

At Mass one morning, the priest was sharing that the Pope was thinking about changing the "Our Father" prayer to eliminate the words "lead us not into temptation." I went to the upper room of my mind that morning to talk to Jesus. When I arrived, I looked up at him and asked:

"Why 'lead us not into temptation'? Why would you say that?"

Jesus responded:

"Where do I take you as part of the refinement that you are going through?"

Various tests in both the Spiritual and earthly dimensions that I have endured flashed through my mind confirming the temptations. I continued by asking Jesus why he told the disciples to pray that they not be tested by the refiner's fire but be delivered directly from evil to Our Father.

Jesus replied,
"It is not an easy road."

Bewildered, I looked at him and said, "Yes, I see that now. But it is my road, the one you are taking me on. Why am I on this road while you tell the disciples to pray to be delivered directly to the Father? I like the idea of *'only say the word, and your soul shall be healed.'* (Matthew 8:8)' Being tested is not a pleasant path; in fact, it is utter hell if you want my opinion." Gazing at me with sorrowful eyes, Jesus explained, "I made you specifically for this road and am walking it with you. I love you."

Through Spiritual revelation in Scripture, I came to understand that if Jesus were here, he would not be a priest because of the laws of the gifts which state that a celibate man is the only acceptable individual to become an ordained priest in the Catholic church. I am not entirely sure what the original intent of this Scripture in the book of Hebrews was, but when I read it, I clearly understood that the laws of the Catholic Church had to change before I could become a priestess.

A Better Ministry

Now the main point in what has been said is this: we have such a high priest, who has taken His seat at the right hand of the throne of the Majesty in the heavens, a minister in the sanctuary and in the true tabernacle, which the Lord pitched, not man. For every high priest is appointed to offer both gifts and sacrifices; so it is necessary that this high priest also have something to offer. Now if He were on earth, He would not be a priest at all, since there are those who offer the gifts according to the Law.
—Hebrews 8:1-4

High Priest

18 Survival

I was struggling internally with staying in the Catholic Church. Jesus was holding me there and telling me I was going to have a leadership role. Even though I was frustrated and didn't see a path to accomplish the task, I was determined to remain obedient. The male hierarchy had built themselves a powerful institution, and they were unwilling to listen to a female voice of understanding let alone step down from their lofty platform. I had a dream about cookies one night as I drifted off to sleep:

Dream

The Catholic Church became the bottom chocolate wafer of an Oreo cookie,

holding me up while I am blind to what's happening. I feel disconnected,

yet perceive support—it's a curious relationship.

I am the cream in the middle layer of the cookie without a

clear picture of what I am doing. I feel quite soft and pliable.

Jesus is the lemon wafer on top, holding me together

so I don't crumble, and for whatever reason, keeping me in the Catholic Church

despite insurmountable conflicts cause by closed minds—the work of the antichrist.

My Oreo is symbolic:

The wafer on the top is pure gold; Heaven makes sense; it is love.

I have no idea what people on earth are doing; they make no sense to me.

The bottom wafer is black because I am in the dark.

I look right at Heaven and keep my **eyes fixed**

on Jesus. It's how I survive.

I listen, not speak, to hear Heaven clearly and directly everywhere.

I reprove and discipline those whom I love. Be earnest, therefore, and repent. Listen! I am standing at the door, knocking; if you hear my voice and open the door, I will come into you and eat with you, and you with me. To the one who conquers I will give a place with me on my throne, just as I myself conquered and sat down with my Father on his throne. Let anyone who has an ear listen to what the Spirit is saying to the churches.
—Revelation 3: 19-22

Cookies and Milk

19 Sprout

Isaiah 11:1
A shoot will come up
from the stump of Jesse;
From his roots a branch
will bear fruit.

Sprout

Continuing with our empty-nester travel excursions, Charles and I went on a Holy Land pilgrimage with our parish. Another opportunity for me to uncover the undiscovered. It was astonishing to be walking on the same ground where Jesus and his disciples walked. As the tour guide provided historical facts, I envisioned what things must have been like during Jesus's time on earth. It was my attempt to bring history to life in real time.

Revelation frequently manifests during visualization—current revelation that transforms time into history in the making. I often perceive that I am doing Heaven's work on earth without knowing how—the result of turning my life over to Jesus. I was anticipating that something profound would happen while I was in the Holy Land, but only one mystical event transpired during the entire pilgrimage.

Our pilgrimage group walked through the Garden of Gethsemane and stopped at an olive tree that was completely fenced in. The tree had an enormous trunk and one new sprout growing. The guide informed us that the tree was the only one left in the garden that was thought to be old enough to be present during Jesus' time. According to the guide, it's believed that Jesus leaned against the tree before his passion. The tour guide explained that the tree had been barren until fifty-one years ago when a new sprout emerged. At those words, I stopped dead in my tracks, felt my body shudder, and experienced the tingling sensation of the Spirit spreading outward from the base of my spine through my entire body. Thousands of electrifying shocks emanated to my extremities, and I experienced a single instant of the fullness of life in every cell of my body.

I was fifty-one years old.

Peace for the Disciples

I have said these things to you in figures of speech. The hour is coming when I will no longer speak to you in figures, but will tell you plainly of the Father. On that day you will ask in my name. I do not say to you that I will ask the Father on your behalf; for the Father himself loves you, because you have loved me and have believed that I came from God. I came from the Father and have come into the world.
—John 16:25–28

20 Name Written in Heaven

Military Bus

Dream

I sit alone on the top level of a large double-decker military bus with men yelling below, my khaki work coat on the floor, books scattered about, and notes sprawled everywhere. My mind is working hard to block the men out while I am piecing clues together as I scribble notes trying to work humanity's puzzle to a conclusion. Having seen several trajectories for the human race in visions that didn't end well, I am beginning to consider that the extinction of our race is imminent.

The bus driver calls out, "It's the Buffalo stop." I gather my stuff up and walk down the stairs and exit the bus without looking back at the yelling men. I head into the wilderness, the great unknown, unaware of what's ahead or even where I am. Wearing my oversized military coat, I enter a large outdoor market. My father and brother are talking me through what's coming next. I listen while others scramble around me, hellbent on distracting me from completing my assignment. As I push forward, I notice my father and brother are gone. I'm not sure where they went, but I can feel my heart rate increasing. I proceed with elevated caution. My eyes open wide as I approach a sea full of men, and suddenly my radar is flying above. I walk cautiously forward, checking overhead to determine the intent of the masses that part as I cross. I gather needed information and proceed out of the tent.

The tribe gathers around the fire—a herd of men and just me. My father and brother are nowhere in sight. I sit at the head of the circle, but the men all think they know best, so I head to the quarry on my own for needed rest. I step into a small rowboat and lower myself to the bottom of the quarry using the strength of my mind.

When I leave the quarry, I enter a cave and stand before a council to answer questions. There are five or six young girls off to the right covered in dark clothes with black lace draped over their heads. I can't see the girls' faces. There is a crowd of men off to the left peering through the forest at me as I stand before the council. They are all smoking and awaiting my answer. Unwilling to leave women covered in darkness, I answer that I will push forward on the crusade. I will do what is necessary to shed light.

Beloved: A Poem of Contradiction

Your name written in heaven means you're destined to suffer.

I came down from above to pour out my love, yet I brace myself daily.

Open Scripture as a safeguard, then walk forward blindfolded and silenced.

To the netherworld, I sink—a tumultuous path.

It seems too familiar. Have I been here before?

I am confident I have, but it's out of my grasp.

Everyone is mad; they need something from me.

Why won't I deliver when so much could be done?

They say I have powers that need to be tapped.

How do I deliver what they want when I haven't excavated what I've got?

The pressure's too much, the rules undefined, I refuse to move forward with my life

in rewind.

Ignored for so long, and now I'm THE ONE?

This life is bizarre—I wasn't trying to be a star.

Leave me alone—I would rather go home.

My savior is gentle, and I'm acceptable as me.

This world, most definitely, is not what I need.

Star

I ponder what surrounds me, wanting everything correct.

Do I have what is needed to make us all intersect?

"Woe to you, Chorazin! Woe to you, Bethsaida! For if the mighty deeds done in your midst had been done in Tyre and Sidon they would long ago have repented, sitting in sackcloth and ashes. But it will be more tolerable for Tyre and Sidon at the judgment than for you. And as for you, Capernaum, 'will you be exalted to heaven? You will go down to the netherworld.' Whoever listens to you listens to me." Whoever rejects you rejects me. And whoever rejects me rejects the one who sent me. The seventy (two) returned rejoicing, and said, "Lord, even the demons are subject to us because of your name." Jesus said, "I have observed Satan fall like lightning from the sky. Behold, I have given you the power to 'tread upon serpents' and scorpions and upon the full force of the enemy and nothing will harm you. Nevertheless, do not rejoice because the spirits are subject to you, but rejoice because your names are written in heaven."
—Luke 10:13–20

21 When Does Marriage Start?

Some Pharisees came to Jesus, testing Him and asking, "Is it lawful for a man to divorce his wife for any reason at all?" And He answered and said, "Have you not read that He who created them from the beginning made them male and female, and said, 'For this reason a man shall leave his father and mother and be joined to his wife, and the two shall become one flesh'? So they are no longer two, but one flesh. What therefore God has joined together, let no man separate."
—Matthew 19:3-6

It's Black and White

The answer popped right into my mind;

How could I have been so blind?

Written before me in black and white

While we carry on as if God's answer is out of sight.

A marriage starts when two bodies unite:

Official documents or words spoken from the altar

Don't replace the laws of nature.

Bible

The freedom many now seize

To lie where they please

Spawn ailments that alter our species structure,

Causing obstacles to be encountered before a marriage starts.

The human ego now large,

We ignore a simple charge.

Only God could comprehend

How things would end.

There is no veil to be lifted.

The Scripture plainly states

God's direct orders, which worldly laws obliterate.

How did I know what others couldn't see?

Years of study, practice, and a Ph.D.—

They had absolutely nothing on me.

The answer printed right on the page,

Yet God's command still overlooked from age to age.

Stepping out on untouched snow,

I try to share what all should know.

Creating a path to shine Christ's light,

Helping all reach monumental heights.

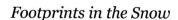

Footprints in the Snow

A Holy Family only happens when a Virgin Bride marries a Godly Man.

Holy Union

22 Love Triangle

Why exactly is love so often a triangle?

I was sinning and didn't even know it.

Was I married to Buck because he was my first?

As I pondered the revelation of marriage starting when a man and woman consummate their union, rather than when the government or church declares a couple married, my mind zipped back to something a neighbor disclosed to me a few years ago. She was on her second marriage and shared with me that her first husband was an actor who played the Marlboro Man in the cigarette commercials decades ago. Her story reminded me that my first love, Buck, smoked Marlboros when we were kids. In fact, that's how I started smoking—taking drags off Buck's cigarette while he unsuccessfully tried to teach me how to make smoke rings.

Marlboro

I knew in an instant: God considered Buck my husband. The humanmade laws of the church and government didn't trump God's mandates. Whose laws do I follow: God's laws or those of the authorities on earth who think they make the rules? The heavens declare me not only a sinner—Mary Magdalene—but also an adulteress.

Merge

I am not a widow based on God's Divine laws.

Buck tossed me aside while holding my heart tight.

Charles poured out love on the pieces remaining,

but sadly, my heart was severely bleeding.

An adulteress I am declared,

but I didn't understand that the rules of the universe

locked me out of the Promised Land.

If I were in charge, every person would find

the soulmate God intended.

Then when their flesh met, two minds would connect.

Merging Heaven and earth,

A union creating a nation offering rebirth.

For a married woman is bound by law to her husband while he lives, but if her husband dies, she is released from the law of marriage. Accordingly, she will be called an adulteress if she lives with another man while her husband is alive. But if her husband dies, she is free from that law, and if she marries another man, she is not an adulteress.
—Romans 7:2–3

23 Eye of the Needle

And Jesus said to His disciples, "Truly I say to you, it is hard for a rich man to enter the kingdom of heaven. Again I say to you, it is easier for a camel to go through the eye of a needle, than for a rich man to enter the kingdom of God." When the disciples heard this, they were very astonished and said, "Then who can be saved?" And looking at them Jesus said to them, "With people this is impossible, but with God all things are possible."
—Matthew 19:23–26

Eye of the Needle

Revelation continued to flow powerfully through me after our return from the Holy Land. As I contemplated who exactly I was and what my job might entail, dreams and visions of passing through the eye of the needle and entering God's Kingdom came daily—the sacred passage of two beloveds as they enter the Kingdom and become whole.

I was tormented daily speculating how I would thread the eye of the needle without hurting anyone. Not only was I not sure who I was married to anymore, but I was also concerned that the rest of my loved ones were unaware that they were sinning and losing access to their Promised

Land. The majority of humanity was squandering their opportunity to live the fullness of life because they didn't understand when a marriage started. I was convinced that this misunderstanding was why the blood vessels in my brain had turned into what Jesus calls a babble knot that locked me out of the Promised Land.

As I jogged down the road next to the curb early one morning, I heard some ladies talking in my temple trying to guide me through the eye of the needle with my heavenly husband. They were quite annoyed with me and losing patience. But I refused to leave anybody I loved behind. It just felt wrong—irresponsible and selfish. I turned the music up to drown out the ladies' "heavenly voices." I don't know what the consequences are for being stubborn in "the heavens." I suppose I will find out one day if they ever decide to let me in on my terms …

Entrance to God's Kingdom

Thread the eye of a needle   not humanly possible

But somehow, I see it as easy   Who does that make me?

I am lucidly being lured in,   but something deters me.

Did I collect what we need   to make straight our pass?

I refuse to leave anyone   behind—merely to suffer

when we all can be whole   and live life to the fullest.

To cleanse and nurture my   mission. It's not time to rise.

Instead I must hide,   here underground, until

all humanity has the opportunity

to gain freedom on land!

24 The World Became Silent

Floating above the World

Only then, my master told me, when you have rejected the deceiver, can you pass through the hardest gate of all, to attain the fifth bough and the fruit of clarity and truth. Only then will you know the clarity and truth of your soul and, knowing yourself for the first time, understand that you are a child of the living spirit. And as my soul moved upward, I realized that I could no longer hear the voice of the world, as all had become as silence.
—Gospel of Mary Magdalene 42:10

Standing Out

It was toward the end of my fourth year in heaven's virtual prison that literally everything in **the world made perfect sense to me.**

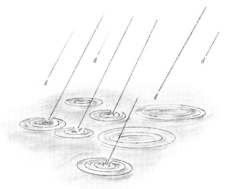

The World Became Silent

The number of raindrops on my windshield matched the continuity of nature, the number of ants marching across the sidewalk was in Divine order, and the number and color of leaves falling off the oak tree were aligned with the universal tapestry. I could see everything from such a granular view that nothing was a coincidence.

Not a single thing failed to connect to the whole for me.

People were no longer individuals, but I saw how all their beings connected to the whole; I was able to separate Divine parts from pieces that needed to be removed before each object and person could be united to the aggregate.

I viewed the whole from above.
The world became utterly silent, and my body radiated in a tingling pattern
from the inside out. I was most certainly floating with the Divine farther out in the
universe than I had before.

How did I get all the way out here?

Can anyone else see what I can see?

Am I still on earth?

Or maybe in Heaven floating around with God?
I am not quite sure.
I have been sitting in Heaven sporadically for years now,
sometimes not realizing I was there, and at other times,
my senses made it clear that I was.

Falling Leaves

But this was more obscure than I am comfortable with.

**Jesus said to me once that he didn't create me
to fit in but to stand out.**

This was standing way out.

I heard a voice in my ear not long after I "stood out" say the words "from empty human eyes
to all-seeing eyes." I am undecided whether either of those extremes is a blessing; all-seeing eyes
would be better than empty ones, I suppose. I seem to see and understand more about Heaven
than most people I encounter. It's a blessing and a curse at the same time. I don't remember when
I was able to connect everything with my feet on the ground, but I am more comfortable with that
version of Divine knowledge.

It was the summer of 2017 when I became obsessed with understanding who Mary Magdalene was to Jesus and to the world. Why had the world discounted her for so long when it was
clear to me that she mattered to the world. I decided to head to the south of France during the
feast of Mary Magdalene and venture to Sainte Baume to the Grotto of Mary Magdalene, where
she supposedly lived after Jesus ascended to Heaven. It was there that she was taken up to Heaven
for nourishment for a reported thirty-three years.

It was around this same time that my "adopted" brother, Byron, resurfaced in my life. Byron dated my sister for a short stretch when they were in high school. All the boys loved Julee and wanted to date her. Byron, and her other boyfriends who came and went, liked me as if I was their squirrely little sister. They teased me, and I batted right back at them; they treated me like one of the boys, for the most part. I fit right in, but they spared me from compliance with the "boy rules." I could get away with anything, and nobody would mess with me when they were around—I was protected.

When Byron and Julee broke up, my mom kept watch over him, and he ended up a fixture at our house for years to come. My mom took in every stray who came around because Mom had a heart of gold, and Byron needed saving coming from a highly dysfunctional family. Byron eventually went into the Marines and even had duty guarding the president for a stint.

Byron had a crush on me one summer when I was in high school and he was home on military leave staying at our house in Fairview, Pennsylvania. He reminded me of this recently. Why? I wasn't sure, but I wasn't surprised that he had come out of the woodwork all of the sudden like so many of my old friends have in recent years. What was odd was that he had recently lived in Charlotte for three years, only a few miles from me, married to a woman named Amy. Byron had "Amy" tattooed on his arm. He knew I lived in Charlotte and never looked me up during the three years he lived there. A coincidence? Not likely. It made me wonder how many people exactly are circling me. Byron and I texted back and forth during my trip to France, reminiscing about old times. I had the sinking suspicion that Byron was babysitting me as if I needed a big "brother" watching me. And as annoyed as I was about being watched, I decided that if I had to have somebody watching me, I was glad it was Byron. I didn't feel judged, and I felt protected; Byron was a marine.

On the bright side, I convinced my girlfriend, Bonnie, to go with me to France. Bonnie is adventurous and was up for traveling with me on a whim. We landed in Nice and spent a few days exploring the French Riviera, which was breathtaking. We continued along the coast to Monaco, and while it was alluring, I was not impressed with the exclusivity of the city. Crowds of tourists stood in front of a casino gawking at expensive cars, hoping to see famous people, but were not welcomed in unless they were "somebody." Honestly, I didn't need to see that shit. I have no interest in seeing what the rich and famous can enjoy when I am not entitled to enter the building. Give me a break. I would rather have fun than look at what I can't do that others can—seriously obnoxious. I would prefer to go mudding with some good old boys in a pickup truck while listening to good music and drinking a beer. We didn't stay in Monaco long, we headed to Sainte Baume.

When Bonnie and I got to Sainte Baume, I fell in love. The Cathedral of Mary Magdalene and the Grotto were beautiful. Most importantly, people in small towns in the south of France seem to understand the true value of a woman. The story of Jesus, Mary, and Joseph is told in an entirely different way there than in the US. It is clearly believed that Mary and Jesus were married and had children based on the plaques in the churches, the shrines, and my understanding of the beliefs they followed.

The village of Saint Baume was small and simple, but charming, and I felt entirely at home. One night after we went to bed, I heard an insane amount of commotion; I listened to the rumbling engines of hundreds of trucks entering the sleepy town and loud construction going on all night long. When we woke the next morning, there was an enormous outdoor flea market set up.

It was unbelievable. Bonnie slept through the whole thing! The immensity of the flea market when we strolled the streets the next morning was incredible! OMG, the biggest flea market I have ever seen in my life. Bonnie and I had a ball. We ate fresh peaches for breakfast and drooled over the olive and almond spreads that several vendors displayed. Talk about a miraculous overnight production.

We made a few stops after leaving Saint Baume, including the city of two Marys, where they were surprised to see us because tourists don't generally visit. It's a vacation spot for locals. Our visit to the city of two Marys made me think that I am "Mary" for the second time. The Blessed Mary before and now Mary Magdalene pouring out my purity to save my children from the walk-through hell that I was taking. At the time, it was just a consideration oscillating through my mind: that I would never leave a child behind but circle for an eternity until I gathered them all—the life of a Mother.

Before leaving France, Bonnie and I headed back to the Grotto of Mary Magdalene for the pilgrimage of the feast of Mary Magdalene on July 22. Nothing profound happened other than my feeling at home in the cave when I shouldn't have. The cave was dark and damp and propagated isolation, loneliness, and heartbreak inside me. I felt as though Jesus was my love, and I was the one trapped in the cave for an eternity trying to figure out how to save Him, unable to comprehend how any living species was reduced to such evil.

Outdoor Market

Grotto of Mary Magdalene

25 Desolation and the Little White Church

To see things and not understand what they are about, or when they might happen, is disturbing. My fourth year experiencing relentless cycles moving from darkness to light in heaven's virtual prison was coming to an end.

I felt shackles on my ankles,

and what lay ahead each day was utterly unknown.

Until one day when I received a prophetic message from an angel letting me know that I would soon enter a virtual "office." What exactly that meant and how I received the message, I cannot explain. Some things come by osmosis—I just know.

What I was starting to understand and see distinctly was what specifically I should be writing down without being terrified that the events would be happening to me. Rather, they were prophetic messages.

Spiral Notebook and Pen

Charles and I had gone to a local sports bar to eat wings and watch a New England Patriots football game one warm fall afternoon when the Spirit was funneling through me. I knew the Spirit was moving because of the smell of incense in the restaurant. After the football game, we decided to go for a Sunday drive through the countryside. Charles recommended I bring along my camera and snap some pictures. While it seemed like an odd request at the time, I soon figured out that he wanted me to understand I was seeing things nobody else could see. As we drove through the countryside in Waxhaw, I saw the aftermath of a cataclysm. The farms had been wiped out, homes that used to be there were gone, corner gas stations were reduced to piles of rubble and concrete, and the rolling hills and fields were burned to ash—complete desolation.

My eyes grew wide as I held my camera outside the convertible top snapping photographs. I was distraught by what I was seeing. When would this happen, or had it already happened? Who burned down the buildings and fields? It was sad; I loved farms and the openness of the rolling fields with horses grazing, all neatly fenced in. Everything was destroyed. By what, I had no idea.

At the end of our afternoon drive, I glanced off to the right side of the road, and a single small white church was still standing. The church had a cute portico at the front and a single white steeple with a bell at the top. The only building left in Waxhaw. A beautiful sight after what felt like a drive through hell. Everything wiped out except one perfect white church.

When I arrived home, I quickly plugged my camera into my computer to view the pictures and discovered that what I had seen with my eyes was not even close to what the camera captured. The images my camera captured were exactly what I viewed in Waxhaw a few days prior when the Spirit

Desolation and the Little White Church

was not flowing through me; the houses, gas stations, farms, and fields were all intact. Bewildered, my mind started to click fast, pulling various pieces of information from the past together, and I am pretty sure I said out loud:

"I am being mind-raped!"

The gods in the heavens are spinning me in circles to get information out of my head ... and Charles is helping them! How else would he know to have me take pictures so I would realize my vision was different than the rest of the world when the Spirit was flowing through me? Rattled, I sat at my kitchen island staring at my computer screen. Everything I understood to be true for decades was now in question, including my identity. Who am I that I can see what others cannot?

Charles came into the house after smoking his cigar, and I started to explain to him that

the pictures I took on our drive were different from what I saw with my eyes. I debated out loud whether that was why God told me a few years ago that I was his arm on earth—because I see things others do not. I am uncertain if they are views of the future, views of the past, parallel views of alternate realities, or possibly a metaphorical view of what is happening today.

Charles looked at me and asked if I thought I was using my index finger to point at the answers, or if maybe there was an army working on God's behalf feeding the information into my mind. Anger rose in me, and I responded with as much restraint as I could that NO, I was quite positive I was living like a caged animal, being held in the white tent I see in my visions. I am being "mind-raped" regularly to get Heavenly information out of my mind, which seems to be considered the holy grail by the gods in the heavens—like E.T. sitting in King David's tent, except I have virtual chains holding me and release is not an option. I am like an extraterrestrial being poked and prodded to extract revelation; some individuals were trying to help me get home while others were afraid of me and wanted to harm me. The big difference between my story and the movie E.T. is that there is no Eliot luring me to his home with Reese's pieces or saving me by putting me in the basket of his bicycle for an exhilarating ride through the sky, finally finding my way home. Instead, I am running around the universe, blindfolded, gagged, and chained, finding needed answers because, at the end of the day, they can't do jack shit without me. Charles did not respond to my rant. He simply stared blankly at me, then returned to the outdoor room to continue smoking his cigar. I was used to not only Charles, but everybody being nonresponsive to what I considered words of enlightenment and wisdom. The world could no longer comprehend me; not what I saw, heard, or understood. It seemed to scare them.

I am confident my life is not my own: I am merely a voodoo doll being poked, prodded, and used as a lab rat, and my husband is a part of this so-called army extracting information out of the ark in my head against my will. Charles suggesting that it was God's army doing the work and that I was just a flow-through vessel infuriated me.

If I am of no value, then why are they bothering with me at all?
They can get everybody into the Promised Land on their own.
Find another ark to pillage, and kill me.
I, most certainly, am not enjoying myself.

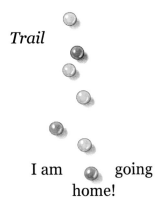

Trail

I am   going home!

Suddenly, I felt incredibly angry and violated. My mind is a looking glass and a camera, and I am an ark being plundered. My life has been sacrificed to gather information for the greater good, so my treasure must be in Heaven. It certainly is not here.

How can this end faster?

Now these are the words of the scroll which Baruch, son of Neriah, son of Mahseiah, son of Zedekiah, son of Hasadiah, son of Hilkiah, wrote in Babylon, in the fifth year, on the seventh day of the month, at the time the Chaldeans took Jerusalem and destroyed it with fire. Baruch read the words of this scroll in the hearing of Jeconiah, son of Jehoiakim, king of Judah, and all the people who came to the reading: the nobles, kings' sons, elders, and all the people, small and great—all who lived in Babylon by the river Sud.

They wept, fasted, and prayed before the Lord, and collected such funds as each could afford. These they sent to Jerusalem, to Jehoiakim the priest, son of Hilkiah, son of Shallum, and to the priests and the whole people who were with him in Jerusalem. At the same time he received the vessels of the house of the Lord that had been removed from the temple, to restore them to the land of Judah, on the tenth of Sivan. These silver vessels Zedekiah, son of Josiah, king of Judah, had made after Nebuchadnezzar, king of Babylon, carried off as captives Jeconiah and the princes, the skilled workers, the nobles, and the people of the land from Jerusalem, and brought them to Babylon.
—Baruch 1:1–9

26 Cup of Suffering

I heard another voice from heaven, saying, "Come out of her, my people, so that you will not participate in her sins and receive of her plagues; for her sins have piled up as high as heaven, and God has remembered her iniquities. Pay her back even as she has paid and give back to her double according to her deeds; in the cup which she has mixed, mix twice as much for her. To the degree that she glorified herself and lived sensuously, to the same degree give her torment and mourning; for she says in her heart, 'I sit as a queen and I am not a widow, and will never see mourning.' For this reason in one day her plagues will come, pestilence and mourning and famine, and she will be burned up with fire; for the Lord God who judges her is strong." Lament for Babylon: And the kings of the earth, who committed acts of immorality and lived sensuously with her, will weep and lament over her when they see the smoke of her burning, standing at a distance because of the fear of her torment, saying, "Woe, woe, the great city, Babylon, the strong city!"
—Revelation 18:4–10

Suffering

To be handed a cup and not understand what it means.
To lose your parents when you've not yet grown up.
To have your heart broken with no way to mend it.
To be abandoned by family without any explanation.
To feel an emotion and be unable to express it.
To hear a voice give directions when nobody is present.
To spin in circles, surrounded by darkness.
To vomit inexplicably for years as you stumble through pandemonium.
To live in confusion, unsure of your trajectory.
To look through people and see their demons while navigating the world.
To endure repeated rejection, leading to loneliness.

To see what others can't, no confirmation ever made.

To be virtually shackled and chained, feeling things unseen.

To not meet your captors but understand their distant orders.

To sit in isolation with no hand to grasp.

To try to run away when there's nowhere to hide.

To be fed false information and asked to determine the truth.

To step outside your body, to turn and look back.

To reside above the world, unable to join the community.

To watch the weather change in conjunction with your mood.

To take photos of your surroundings that don't match your view.

To know the answer when nobody will listen.

To have something to say but be unable to speak.

To be told how you should feel instead of asked what you're experiencing.

To suffer Christ's wounds and become accustomed to pain.

To worry you are hurting someone and not know how to stop it.

To watch your sister fade with no way to fix her.

To be assigned an undefined job where the rules constantly change.

To carry the weight of the world, not knowing the end goal.

To be isolated in exile for countless years on end.

To face your truth after being turned upside down.

Jesus handed me a gold chalice one day when I was sitting in the upper room of my mind. At the time, I thought it was a beautiful gift. I was going to sit right next to Jesus and serve His people from behind the altar. I didn't understand what it would mean to suffer for the cross by drinking from the cup I was handed. I knew that I loved him and was willing to do his work, no matter the cost. But when I was given the cup of suffering, how long I would suffer and what I would bear was entirely out of my grasp. Why was I chosen? I wasn't supposed to ask, but still, I pondered.

I surmised I was hidden underground for safekeeping, and now it was my turn to suffer—do my job. The exact job description and requirements I was not privy to. But, I spotted a sign at a craft fair that read, "God doesn't call the qualified; He qualifies the called." I quickly gathered that my eternal suffering was meant to qualify me to do my job. A job that entailed intermittent days of physical darkness and unusual weather patterns, along with unnatural and sometimes terrifying mystical occurrences. These eerie experiences were tucked between periods of the peace of Jesus Christ and stretches of calmness during which I was surrounded and comforted by Heaven's angels.

The predictions in the passage from Revelation did not make me feel good but they certainly worked given my life experiences. I could easily fit the pieces of my life into the puzzle I was building in Bible Scripture. As it says in the Revelation Scripture, people in my life indeed have abandoned me and stand at a distance. I have what Jesus calls a babble knot or cluster of blood vessels in my brain that was discovered in 1999 when I was ill, and I am holding a gold chalice in Heaven when I meditate in the upper room of my mind.

The icing on the cake, which happens to be my favorite part:

Jesus Christ showed up and said He would fix me.

"Father, if You are willing, remove this cup from Me; Let not My will, but Yours be done."
—Luke 22:42

Birthday Cake

27 Your Sister's Cup

You have gone the way of your sister; therefore, I will give her cup into your hand. Thus, says the Lord God You shall drink your sister's cup, which is deep and large; you shall be laughed at and held in derision, for it contains much; you will be filled with drunkenness and sorrow. A cup of horror and desolation is the cup of your sister Samaria; you shall drink it and drain it out, and pluck out your hair, and tear your breasts; for I have spoken says the Lord God. Because you have forgotten me and cast me behind your back, therefore bear the consequences of your lewdness and harlotry.
—Ezekiel 23:31–35

We all suffer for others; it's part of the plan, to lift one another up when they need a hand. Now my sister is short—only five-foot-one—and often I would tell her about things above us or reach high places to pull down what she couldn't.

The two of us joke about how completely opposite we are. Not a bad plan as she fills in where I lack, and I, in return, do the same thing back. My sister speaks freely with kind words to all, and frequently, she would speak a few words for me.

My height was my advantage, and I was physically agile, so it was best not to mess with my sister, or you would deal with me. I was stubborn and silent, but I rarely missed a thing. Those who broke through would learn new things.

My sister's MS and inability to breathe have plagued much of her life with unimaginable pain. My recent encounters with heaven and hell have left me in exile for too many years. Who is suffering more is an unanswerable question, but drinking a cup of suffering is a horrific task!

Neither one of us was untouched, the day we walked down the aisle; so clearly, both harlots, as described in the Bible. Thankfully we are Daughters tucked under Heaven's umbrella, protected by a promise that ends in salvation.

Heaven's Umbrella

28 Love Telegraph from Exile

For my own name's sake I delay my wrath;
for the sake of my praise I hold it back from you,
so as not to destroy you completely.
See, I have refined you, though not as silver;
I have tested you in the furnace of affliction.
For my own sake, for my own sake, I do this.
How can I let myself be defamed?
I will not yield my glory to another.
"Listen to me, Jacob,
Israel, whom I have called:
I am he;
I am the first and I am the last.
My own hand laid the foundations of the earth,
and my right hand spread out the heavens;
when I summon them,
they all stand up together.
—Isaiah 48: 9-13

Entering year four of my exile, while spinning through a cleansing cycle,
I rummaged through my attic.

I found boxes of old pictures, cards, school records, and letters. I carefully pulled my old memories out of the box and thought back on carefree days and old friends. I came across an envelope that had two letters from my high school and college boyfriend, Buck, and a picture of us when we were in high school. Tears started rolling down my cheeks as I stared at the picture. I cried, my eyes fixed on the photograph, while my mind shifted back in time. It was not often that a tear graced my cheek, but the ache in my heart over the loss remained all these years later.

Love Telegraph from Exile

There was only a brief period in the last twenty-eight years when I didn't think about Buck or search for him in my dreams at night; it was in the aftermath of my neurologic illness in 1999. I didn't cry, dream, or feel much emotion for decades. As a result of the illness, Buck seemed to finally be expunged from my thoughts and dreams.

**And I was thankful because
thinking about Buck distracted me
from living fully in the present.**

As I sat staring at the picture, I journeyed back in my mind to when Buck and I met. It was my junior year of high school, I was sixteen, almost seventeen. My girlfriend Kim and I were driving the loop of the public dock parking area in Erie the first time I saw him. Buck was six-foot-four, with broad shoulders and the classic short feathered back hair boys wore in the Eighties. He was standing on the side of the road wearing a leather jacket and blue jeans with his friend Ron. I was instantly attracted to Buck.

Kim and I parked, got out of the car, and walked along the sidewalk toward them. We decided to casually walk past as if we didn't notice them standing there. Buck's friend Ron was maybe five-foot-six with red hair and bright eyes, and he held himself with confidence. Ron hollered out to us, and we walked over and introduced ourselves. After maybe twenty minutes, they had to head home to make curfew.

**Before they left,
Ron invited us to a party
at his house the next weekend;
his parents would be out of town.**

As Kim and I drove home that night, I tried to push Buck out of my mind. It didn't seem to me that he had any interest in me whatsoever. If he did, he didn't let on. Buck was the handsomest boy I had ever met, and something about being near him made me nervous. I had dated a few boys, but I'd never felt like this before. I couldn't pinpoint what it was, but the feeling was exhilarating. In fact, excitingly dangerous. I told myself Buck could probably date anybody he wanted and was definitely out of my league.

Kim and I decided we would go to Ron's party the next weekend. Ron and Buck attended the all-boys Catholic high school. We knew several of the Catholic boys would be at the party. The boys from our public school didn't interest us.

We were certain the boys
from the Catholic school were cuter,
smarter, and more fun.

When we arrived at Ron's house, the place was packed with Catholic school kids—standing room only. We pushed our way through the crowd looking for Ron and Buck. Kim stopped to talk to a boy she knew and had a crush on. I stood with them, listening to them chat. Feeling like a third wheel, I glanced around looking for Buck or Ron, but didn't see them.

I was starting to feel uncomfortable when I spotted Buck. His broad shoulders, high cheekbones, and neatly slicked-back hair, along with his confident gait, were heading right toward me. My heart started to beat out of my chest, and my mind began racing, trying to decide what to say. I wanted to be flirtatious like other girls who knew what they were doing when it came to boys—without looking like an airhead or coming off too giddy like many popular girls did. I hadn't dated much because I was busy being a kid—I was not in a rush to grow up.

I was independent and self-reliant
like my Dad raised me to be.

I was annoyed with myself that I was allowing anyone to make me feel this way—conscious of how I should act and what I should say. There was a loss of control inside of me that teetered between exhilaration and terror; it was that fight-or-flight feeling. The intensity confused me, but the pull of dangerous excitement overpowered my normal rational thinking, which would have led me directly to a flight response.

I was pleasantly surprised when my name came out of Buck's mouth as he walked up to me. A flicker of hope that maybe he was interested in me. Buck started the conversation with the typical small talk you make the first time you meet someone. Where are you from? How many brothers and sisters do you have? What do you do in your spare time? And so on. As we talked and exchanged pleasantries, I began to relax. I was surprised that someone so handsome could be so down to Earth and easy to talk to; it was like we had known each other forever.

A feeling of belonging settled in me
faster than I had expected.

As we continued to talk, Buck seemed vulnerable and open, which surprised me. He was on the football team but didn't get to play much. He was the seventh of nine children, with five older sisters, one older brother, and two younger brothers—a good Catholic family. Buck informed me that he didn't have a car of his own and currently was grounded from driving. He was so honest and raw about who he was. While his sincerity startled me, I felt myself being drawn in. I wondered if Buck was like this with everyone or if he felt unusually at ease with me as I did with him.

I felt myself start to relax as our conversation continued. Buck took a step closer to me, and I leaned in to listen intently. Everyone and everything else in the room quickly faded into the background, and the world started to close in around the two of us. I can't tell you who else was at that party, how long I was there, or what went on that night. I was thoroughly captivated by this handsome boy. Buck resembled the actor Christopher Reeves:

Superman
standing right in front of me.

We talked for several hours, and it was getting late. People were starting to push past us to leave for the night. As a group of kids approached us heading to the door, Buck placed his hand gently on my lower back, pulling me toward him and out of the way of the passing crowd. When he laid his hand on my lower back, the base of my spine trembled, sending a vibration that electrified every inch of my body.

That was it for me; I was in love. Madly in love.

I'm confident that Buck didn't know he was in love with me right away. But we would date for almost six years. We did all the typical high school and college romance things: We had our song ("I Can't Hold Back" by Survivor), talked on the phone for hours, and had some typical teenage breakup and get-back-together drama. Buck made me a wooden plaque that said, "I CAN'T HOLD BACK" AMY I LOVE YOU! and mounted his high school ring in the middle. His ring had a big red stone, which made me think he gave me his heart, and I gave him mine, because he wore my high school ring, which also displayed a red stone, on a chain around his neck.

Buck would break up with me three times during our years together; I would be crushed and then take him back when he poured his heart out to me, asking for a reunion after explaining the reasons for his stupidity. We spent years of youthful bliss parking at the railroad tracks, going to the beach, dressing up for high school proms, blowing off our friends to be alone together, and sharing many "firsts" with one another. More than our parents would have approved of.

The world revolved around the two of us.
We were madly in love with one another.

My mom had told me years prior that when I grew up, I was going to marry a good Catholic man and have three sons. And she was usually right. I was confident by my senior year of high school that Buck was the one. There was no way I was going to love anyone the way I loved Buck … not ever.

A sudden noise jolted me out of my daydream; the hardwood floor creaked in the Attic room where I sat with the picture of Buck and me in my hand. I looked up to see Charles standing in the doorway and quickly tucked the picture into my pocket. Charles had that concerned look on his face that he often gets now when I am in the refiner's fire. He walked over to the pile of memorabilia from my youth that I had scattered all over the attic room and reached down to grab my hand. He said, "Come on, Amy, you can do this later. Let's go grab some dinner." I smiled and tucked the letters in my pocket, and we headed to dinner.

It was hard to stay in the present moment because
my temple was in full rotation, and
my mind was now opened to the memory of Buck.
After years of hard work pushing the feelings away,
I could feel Buck's presence as if it was yesterday.

I'm not sure what Charles and I talked about at dinner that night. I was anxiously waiting to read Buck's old letters and feeling guilty at the same time. I hadn't seen or spoken to Buck for twenty-eight years; how could I feel this way?

**I remembered my mom telling me that
when you are married to someone,
even thinking about another man is a sin.
I am certainly going to hell.**

I hadn't thought about Buck this much for years, and now he was back at the forefront of my mind. Not that I didn't love my husband; Charles is a great man with a beautiful spirit, and we had a beautiful life together. But there is something about my first love, and something about Buck, that I have never been able to shake.

**Years ago, to remove Buck from my mind,
I once prayed to God to make my love for Buck go away:
Please, God, make me love Charles more.**

That prayer was before my illness in 1999. The loss of emotion that occurred after that neurologic illness made it easy to forget Buck until a few years ago when Jesus showed up and stirred me with his presence. When I was feeling terribly guilty about my thoughts and dreams of Buck, my mom's words would echo through my mind about the sin. I am married to a great man; why can't I get Buck out of my head?

After we got home from dinner,

**Charles headed out back to start a fire.
I was desperate to read the letters from Buck.
I went upstairs, sat on my bed,
and pulled out the two letters Buck wrote me
when we were kids.**

Norman Rockwell

I sat and stared at the picture of us, and my temple started to spin as revelation poured through my mind. Buck is wearing a white shirt, so he is purified and saved by the sacrifice of Jesus Christ. I am wearing black and covered in sin like Mary Magdalene, who needs to be cleansed, forgiven, and saved. The encyclopedias behind my head are just like the rivers of wisdom that flowed into my mind when I was in the hospital a few years back. Above my head on the bookshelf is the book *North and South*, symbolic because my spirit moves from Heaven to earth, frequently and quickly. To the left of Buck's head on the bookshelf is the Bible, *The Way*, and then just by his shoulder is a picture of my dad as a young boy. It crossed my mind that Buck was the way to my truth, the way to find light, and he was drawing me to my Father in heaven.

**Some hope for peace,
relief from this spinning and vomiting
—exile from the world.**

A way to get back to the life I deserve!

Was Buck the one person who understood me entirely and could bring me back to life?

Buck was my first husband, according to God's laws, and he did toss me aside:

"Like a wife forsaken and grieved in spirit, a wife married in youth and then cast off."
—Isaiah 54:6

**For all I knew, Buck could be dead, or alive and happily married,
living a beautiful life, and relieved that he dodged a bullet
when he ditched me! After all, I was recently locked up
in a mental ward,and now I am spinning in circles.
Who would want me? Would I spend the rest of
my life alone, daydreaming about a life that
eludes me? Now, at the age of fifty-one,
I was once again pathetically,
oh so pathetically,
obsessed
with my high school and college boyfriend.**

I slammed the picture down, threw myself back on the bed, and stared at the ceiling. *Breathe, just breathe, Amy,* I told myself. Annoyed, I grabbed the envelope and pulled Buck's letters out. The handwriting on the envelope was familiar, and the slant of the writing reminded me that Buck was left-handed. I could envision him sitting at a desk with his hand curved over the tablet as he wrote. I carefully unfolded the first letter as I sat back up on my bed and took a deep breath. I contemplated, *should I read this, or should I just put it away?*

I read the letter.

Immediately, I was shocked by the date change in the letter. Buck writes that it's May 6, then says no, it's May 7. In all of my conversations with Jesus, May 7 is the only date he has ever given me for our union! While Jesus never says what year, this can't be a coincidence.

Many other phrases in Buck's letter were relevant to the present time. The next words that leapt off the page at me were: "You are not here in spirit." That has certainly been the case for years now as my Spirit seems to exit and reenter my body frequently as I float spiritually around the wilderness. Buck also writes that he is at my house with my mom and that my house is not the same without me there because I am the person who makes it mystical. I felt as though God was talking to me through time and space by means of our old letters. Exactly how, I had not yet figured out.

He wrote in the next sentence of the letter that his parents were going to Toronto for the weekend. How odd, because I had just booked a trip to Toronto to attend a Christ for All Nations Christian conference. What in the world; how can I SEE so many current associations in this letter almost three decades later? I felt like I was telescoping through time and space, forward and backward, unable to reside in one place.

**Maybe I am
in Heaven, and everything
is rolling up into one ball of wax;
time is standing still,
and I am rising above
it.**

The last part of the letter jumped off the page at me: Buck said he was going to try to get me a ride home early.

**It was as though he was talking to me right at that moment
through the words he had written years ago.
I think to myself—that would be awesome!
If Buck can get me out of this spinning hell and exile**

when I have not seen or talked to him for twenty-eight years,
I will forgive all the dumb shit he did when we were kids
and all the dumb shit he will likely do in the future.

If nothing else, I was certain we were connected somehow through time and space. I folded the letter back up, knowing I would read it repeatedly because I sensed there was more there than what met my eyes.

I opened the next letter that Buck gave me when he broke up with me during our senior year of high school to date his old girlfriend. As I began to read the letter, Buck is rambling about why he had to see if things could work out with his old girlfriend because they never resolved their relationship.

My mind instantly returned to the present,
realizing that my current loneliness, combined
with feeling betrayed by Charles, was
clouding my normally rational thought process.

Why was I even thinking about a childhood boyfriend? Look at how immature our relationship was. This was ridiculous. I was married; I needed to get over the feelings of betrayal I felt toward Charles and move on with my life.

Annoyed with myself,
I returned the letters to the envelope and put it
in the top drawer of my nightstand for
safekeeping.

29 Repairer of the Breach

When the king heard the words of the book of the law, he tore his clothes. Then the king commanded Hilkiah the priest, Ahikam the son of Shaphan, Achbor the son of Micaiah, Shaphan the scribe, and Asaiah the king's servant saying, "Go, inquire of the Lord for me and the people and all Judah concerning the words of this book that has been found, for great is the wrath of the Lord that burns against us, because our fathers have not listened to the words of this book, to do according to all that is written concerning us."
—2 Kings 22: 11-13

Now why people ignore the words printed in ink in the Bible is beyond me. Some tell me that I am reading the Bible through different "eyes," which I understand. I have been blessed with eyes to SEE. I see beyond the words on the page and the historical and theological meaning of the Scriptures. The veil has been lifted from the Scriptures by the power of the Holy Spirit, and for me, Scripture is a living, current conversation with God. With that said, some words that the church and the government choose to ignore or twist are printed for all eyes to see—no extraordinary vision is necessary.

As revelation from Heaven flowed through me, I recognized many things the Catholic Church is wrong about. We have gone on for so long with only celibate male priests. This was introduced more than a thousand years after the death of Jesus. Before then, women were priestesses, and male priests could marry. I know the Catholic Church is wrong about celibacy, not only because these things are written in Scripture but also from my conversations in the upper room of my mind with Jesus.

> **So why would I listen to the church now?**
> **Why is anyone, for that matter?**
> **The government is clearly corrupt,**

stripping God from the equation and making so many conflicting human laws that leave everyone at a loss as to what law to follow. The church doesn't follow God's laws written in Scripture, and many of the federal, state, and municipal laws contradict one another. I am distraught to think that I have been living in such ignorance, not bothering to question canon law or the contradictory laws imposed by the governments and municipalities of today. How is anybody supposed to know what to do?

I currently sit in a bubble between heaven and earth exiled from both realities. The wrath I endure in this otherworldly space is unlike any experience in the human sphere. From darkness to light, back and forth, strange occurrences materialize that I strain to comprehend:

Insanity

Leaves dance around me,
gravity is defied,
while the devil tries to distract me.
I smell the fragrance from a garden when others cannot,
I see people others don't
and tune into voices from beyond.
Incense burns around me while spirits surround me.
I walk up a west staircase   and come out in the east.
The weather changes around me, and
people I don't recall claim to have seen me.
Bruises appear on my body   and physical signs
manifest,

indicating heavenly passage

if I can pass this insane test.

Leaves

What is so clear and straightforward in Scripture is so twisted in the world we are living in. Not that I am living wholly anywhere; I move from an exile bubble between heaven and earth to the upper room of my mind, where I talk and 'walk' with Jesus.

95

In a recent conversation, Jesus asked me to divorce Charles and marry him. My current husband was not my first husband, according to Scripture, which clearly states that marriage starts when two flesh become one. If I am candid, this has left me confused about who exactly I am married to. My life in the upper room of my mind that I view with my third eye blind has become as much of a reality for me as the reality I see with my human eyes.

I asked Jesus hundreds of times if he really wanted me to divorce my earthly husband and marry Him. And while it may seem wrong that I would question Jesus, I was having a hard time going against what this world has imposed on me as truths during my lifetime. I was struggling with walking on fresh snow, making my own path in life, and leaving a haven with a husband who had been faithful to me. Hurting someone I loved and breaking my family apart felt painful, even if my sons were grown and out of the house. The thought of change was daunting. And the notion of being on my own after twenty-five years of marriage felt paralyzing.

Then again, I was not on my own, was I? I had Jesus with me, and he never left me. I have been able to find him in the upper room of my mind for years now. I would go back and forth for months to come and suffer internal torture before I would make any move toward divorcing Charles as Jesus requested. One day as I sat with Jesus in the upper room of my mind, he reminded me that to purify women and restore the broken family, I needed to take this step. Do what he was asking me. Jesus's words resonated to the depths of my confused soul. His orders fell in line with the Scripture, and prophecy unveiled to me multiple times throughout my faith journey. But it didn't make it any easier to move forward.

Jesus had told me years prior through revelation in Scriptures that I was Lady Zion, the repairer of the breach. What it meant to be Lady Zion was now beginning to make unbridled sense. My mind had put together enough pieces of information to know that if I am who Jesus Christ says I am, then what I do would make a new covenant for all women restoring many families. I would be purifying women covered in sin because they had the same misunderstanding that I did about when marriage started. And then, I would bridge the gap and repair the breach by divorcing one man and marrying another. Basically, my committing what Scripture considers sins would absolve others from the sin, setting them free.

**One might think,
based on the power of my interaction with Jesus,
I would pick up my cross and get divorced—trust me; I wish I had.
But no, I would circle in my mind, testing the spirits for three
confirmations.**

Additional confirmation came just a few weeks later. It was the end of January 2018, and the refiner overshadowed me and came at me full force. I guess I was not moving fast enough for the spirits in the heavens because I was forced to stare myself right in the face.

Charles and I had gone out to dinner, and when we got home, I sat out back by the fire. I could hear heaven talking to me in my head, and I was responding out loud to the heavenly voices. A spirit was insisting that it was okay for me to show my emotions, that how I felt mattered. I didn't need to keep all my feelings hidden behind my concrete wall.

Expressing emotions is a challenge after living your life for so long in a cage. But something inside me snapped that night. Not only was I being asked to divorce Charles to do the job I was put here to do, but I would also break his heart and make my sons uncomfortable. On top of that, the spirits in the heavens wanted me to show my emotions; they were turned off decades ago, stuck inside, unable to escape.

The insistent spirit wouldn't let up, which agitated me. I became furious that a remote spirit would be making demands on me, but the voices making demands wouldn't relent. I could feel steam beginning to erupt from my mind. I went inside to the kitchen, stood on the counter, and wiped every glass out of the kitchen cabinet. At least fifty glasses were broken all over the kitchen floor. And I was yelling at Buck as I was breaking the glasses. Yes, yelling at my high school and college boyfriend.

Not even two minutes later, an ambulance showed up. It wasn't even possible for Charles to place the call and the ambulance to arrive. They hauled me off to the ER against my will.

**Was I not allowed to show my emotions?
Can I not express myself on earth?
Do I even belong on this planet?**

God says I can express myself if I am not hurting anyone, and I was not. Destroying my own property, yes, but not hurting anyone. I had decades of pent-up anger inside. I needed a release. When was the universe going to let me out of this freaking cage I was trapped in? And that's not the exact F-word I used.

I realize that I must have looked as though I was possessed by an evil spirit as I yelled into the air while breaking glasses everywhere—when in fact there were heavenly spirits telling me that I could show emotions and say what I felt, what I liked, what I didn't like, and what I wanted. It reminded me of the day I told my oldest son, Benjamin, to punch the neighbor boy in the nose as hard as he could because I was done with him being bullied, and Benjamin was too.

**It was a freeing moment for me, breaking all that glass.
A monumental release.**

Then the Lord will guide you always and give you plenty even on the parched land. He will renew your strength, and you shall be like a watered garden, like a spring whose water never fails. The ancient ruins shall be rebuilt for your sake, and the foundations from ages past you shall raise up; "Repairer of the breach," they shall call you, "Restorer of ruined homesteads."
—Isaiah 58:11–12

Breach

30 The World Is Twisted

Broken Glass

Breaking all the glasses landed me in the hospital emergency room. It was early evening when I arrived at the ER; the staff did all the typical vital-sign checks before wheeling me into a room. The ER was overflowing with patients; gurneys filled with patients cluttering the hallways. I quickly surmised that it was entirely possible I was seeing people in the spiritual dimension that others were not based on the sheer number of people scattered in the halls. I decided to put my guard up fast. Self-preservation mode was needed.

At this point, I was not talking to Charles at all; I told him after my last trip to the hospital that if he ever sent me there against my will again, I would leave him. I could see the path that Charles was leading me down; he most certainly had overreacted to my breaking the glasses in our kitchen cabinet. I was not at all amused.

Confirmation that Divine Spirits were surrounding me, and that I was walking in multiple dimensions at the same time, came quickly; I noticed that I could smell the fragrance from Heaven's garden being emitted directly from me. Generally, when I smelled Heaven's perfume, I wasn't sure where it was coming from. Today, I felt the oily spot right at the top of my head and knew the fragrance of Heaven was being emitted from my body. My mom used to get a greasy patch on top of her head, too. Unfortunately, Mom died before her temple was erected, but she smelled beautiful and was beautiful.

Being far less spiritually beautiful than my mom, I frequently contemplate if I am the correct woman for this job; I was never trying to be saintly and didn't even work hard to be righteous. In fact, I kind of like breaking rules. Not essential rules that would hurt someone but the type of rules that are ridiculous to begin with. There are so many that I will table that discussion for now; I could write an entire book about stupid rules. But I thoroughly enjoy breaking absurd rules, it makes me feel like I am getting away with something—just a little harmless adrenaline rush.

Anyway, a nurse or an angel saint came by the room and asked me to go for a walk with her to visit other patients in the hospital. I quickly decided that she was most likely an angel or saint; why would a nurse ask me to go for a walk? That made no sense. We walked in and out of the rooms in the ER, laying our hands on one sick patient after another, spreading our perfume from Heaven's garden to everyone. I was in training to do Heaven's work on earth. I may look like an idiot to the world, but one day, I will make sense and hopefully make a difference in the world. Most likely after I'm dead—that's when people are generally recognized and valued for their contributions to humanity. The purification process has made my life on earth absolute hell; someone should benefit in the end, even if it's not me.

I guess the doctors in the ER were trying to figure out what to do with me because I sat around for hours. Early the next morning, I was sitting in the hallway with a very tall male angel or nurse; we were doing a puzzle that had no borders, which was challenging. Maybe impossible. I'm not sure because we didn't finish it. I was busy noticing that the ER staff was incredibly tall; most were over six feet with many pushing seven feet.

As we were doing the puzzle, the angel nurse asked me what I was mad about. I told him that I simply wanted to get my anger out and express myself. It had been trapped inside for a long time, and I was going to explode. We talked about several things, and then somehow, he brought up the topic of love and who I was married to. I explained that I was confused about who I was married to—Charles, my earthly husband, or Buck, my first and my Heavenly husband. I told the angel nurse that the heavens kept making me think about Buck, and it was disturbing my life.

The male angel nurse suggested that if I was angry at Buck, I could be talking to him through time and space, and we could be creating a Heavenly family through our connection.

WHAT?!

My mind was surely going to explode now. Well, this was news to me because I hadn't seen Buck or talked to him for twenty-eight years. I wasn't sure if he was even alive. And I was angry and yelling at him through time and space? I kind of liked that idea. But this angel nurse, I thought, must be batshit crazy.

The next day, when I woke up in the hospital, I was still in the ER. Doctors still don't seem to know what to do with me. I believe I was the sanest person deemed crazy they had ever encountered, leaving them vacillating between releasing me and admitting me. One doctor told me that I was so confident and specific in my recollection that he wasn't sure what to do. I would have been happy to tell him what to do, but I didn't have the correct piece of paper framed on my wall to make it legal. While the doctors continued to debate my destiny, I opened my Bible randomly to this Scripture: *"For more numerous are the children of the deserted wife than the children of her who has a husband, says the Lord"* —Isaiah 54:1.

Interestingly, Buck is the one who tossed me aside or deserted me when we were young. How could I have more children with him than I have earthly children with Charles? Well, I don't know who these Heavenly children might be or precisely what that means, but I hoped they were not relying on Buck! Clearly, that would be a bad idea. I was curious if this was how things work in Heaven; you can talk to people through your minds and possibly procreate that way? It would make an interesting book at the very least, and it would be incredible if it came to fruition. It would also explain how Mary became "with child," having never "been" with a man.

I scanned my journal while I waited around for the doctors' verdict on what they considered wrong with me. I found an entry in my journal from the previous year that I didn't remember writing:

I spent the night in Heaven in a lucid dream. I was watching TV and listening to a commercial when I heard a voice in my head say that I could send a message to Buck in a different language into the universe, and he would understand it and respond. So, I did. I told Buck everything in my heart, and I heard him say back to me, "I can't live without you."

Was I talking to Buck through time and space? How could this be? Or was it simply a dream of my desire? Why did it feel so real? Charles told me once when I was in a spin cycle that he heard me talking to Buck out loud. I felt bad.

Why must I talk to my past when my present was right in front of me? It's like my past was flowing right into my present and through to the future. I must be living in purgatory, I thought, and my whole life was being rolled up into one big ball.

Am I dead?
Am I alive?
Am I in Heaven?
Or is this hell?

Could I be a soul condemned to wander the universe for an eternity?

I sat in the hospital room thinking that if I was talking to Buck through time and space like the angel nurse indicated, then Buck could be dead or alive. The thought unnerved me, and suddenly I needed to find out. Why could I not get rid of this man? No, not this man; Buck was not much more than a boy the last time I saw him. Why wouldn't he go away?

Maybe God is right.
To heal my soul, I need to revisit my whole life and come to terms with it.
What happened to just say the word and your soul shall be healed?
I seriously want that version of salvation.

Jesus said to them in reply, "You are misled because you do not know the Scriptures or the power of God. At the resurrection they neither marry nor are given in marriage but are like the angels in heaven."
—Matthew 22:29-30

31 Ambidextrous

The hospital authorities decided that I should be locked up in a facility for a week, and I was carted off to a mental-health lockup in Davidson.

I was furious, and that is an understatement. I quickly resolved that when I got out of there, I would pack up and leave my earthly husband.

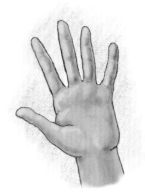

Ambidextrous

The game in the hospital was to frustrate me to see how I would react. I was determined to keep it together, so I could get out of there fast.

I had never thrown anything at anyone. In fact, I have always kept my feelings caged inside, verbally and physically.

Charles was no longer going to have any power to send me to the hospital or sign me in anywhere. I needed control over my life.

I only lost it once. I threw a paper cup at a nurse behind the counter. I don't even remember why, but it landed me in lockup for one extra day.

I am, quite frankly, proud of the fact that I threw that paper cup at her. The nurse was being a bitch; I do remember that.

The fact is the only thing they found wrong with me during my entire stay was that my blood count was down to 7.5.

I had had a female menstrual cycle continuously for four or five months straight and simply hadn't realized how weak I had become from the blood loss.

What incompetent doctors to find me in that physical state, and then lock me up in a facility that did not have a medical doctor.

The therapist on staff confirmed that if I was not a danger to myself or trying to hurt anyone around me, I should not be there.

On a brighter note, it became clear to me while I was locked up that I was ambidextrous while in the spiritual dimension.

In heaven, both hemispheres of my brain worked fully. I could do everything both left- and right-handed: play basketball, write, eat, and brush my teeth.

I was certain I had moved from earth to heaven. I didn't know how I was doing it, but I most definitely was.

Maybe this is the reason it is touted that Mary Magdalene was taken up to Heaven and ministered to by angels for thirty-three years.

It will be thirty-three years from the first time I was stung by a bee in 1987 (which was also the year my mom died) until 2020.

That is when God says I will have perfect vision and go from empty human eyes to all-seeing eyes: wisdom at its height.

While I was locked up, I felt like I was being tortured by spirits as part of the temple-building process going on in my brain.

I was superhuman here and starting to feel fearless again like I did when I was a kid. Nobody visited me while I was imprisoned, and I didn't want to see anyone.

The phone never worked, just like the first time I was locked up. I was challenged daily and frustrated to the point of explosion.

I switched to a self-commitment, so I wouldn't need a judge to get out. I signed myself out after a week and a day.

The extra day, due to my throwing the paper cup at the nurse—that was the best part of my stay. Or maybe the best part was my new basketball skills.

No, throwing the paper cup at the bitch, for sure. I hired a taxi to take me home, where I packed up my belongings and moved into the **Extended Stay America**.

One of the seven angels who had the seven bowls full of the seven last plagues came and said to me, "Come, I will show you the bride, the wife of the Lamb." And he carried me away in the Spirit to a mountain great and high, and showed me the Holy City, Jerusalem, coming down out of heaven from God. It shone with the glory of God, and its brilliance was like that of a very precious jewel, like a jasper, clear as crystal.
Revelation 21: 9-11

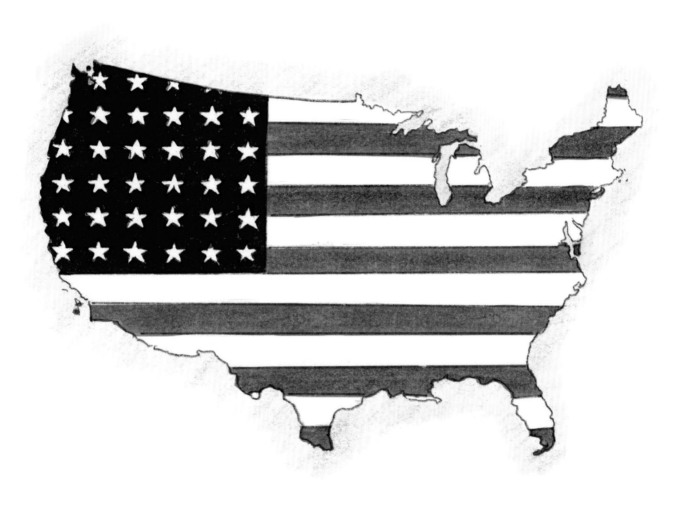

America

32 Companion of My Youth

I was determined to leave my husband, Charles; sending me to the emergency room against my will for the second time was the final straw. A few days after I checked myself out of the hospital, I found an apartment and hired movers. I decided I was taking charge of my life. I cracked open my Bible looking for guidance; I was determined now to listen to what Jesus was telling me: divorce Charles and marry him to purify women and unite the

broken family.

I randomly opened the Bible, and my eyes fell on this:

> *One who forsakes the companion of her youth and forgets the covenant of her God; For her path sinks down to death, and her footsteps lead to the shades.*
> —Proverbs 2:17–18

As I reflected on this Scripture, I decided I needed to find the companion of my youth,

Buck.

God told me years ago that he was going to go get Buck if that's what it took to fix me, and now I was going to do it myself. Jesus said many times that he would make me worthy enough for him to enter under my roof. My soul had to be fixed so this could happen; how else would I do the work of Jesus Christ here on earth? But calling an old flame twenty-eight years later—

Really?
Did I have to do this to fix my soul?
So annoying.

I flipped the pages of my Bible to the second Scripture of my morning prayer, and my eyes landed here:

Come now, let us set things right, says the Lord: Though your sins be like scarlet, they may become white as snow. Though they may be crimson red, they may become white as wool. If you are willing, and obey, you shall eat good things of the land; But if you refuse and resist, the sword shall consume.
—Isaiah 1:18-20

I am ready to be fixed. For things to be set right.
If Jesus Christ is going to fix me, then I am willing.

Scarlet Letter

33 Do I Look Dumb?

The Tower of Babel

Now the whole earth had one language and few words.
—Genesis 11:1

Scattered

People must speculate why I rarely speak
When signs and wonders happen around me each week.

    Words from the heavens flow through my mind,
    making me appear dumb to those who are blind.

      Heavenly information is trapped—there's a cage door in my mind,
      My lips paralyzed until I unwind.
I know what I hear,
      but I can't bridge the gap,
            to verbalize the words—
something holds me back.

      The space that I occupied,
      while being forced to hide,
        kept me from standing
        beyond the divide.

My scattered brain resided in more than one place,
    scouring the universe in an ungodly space.
    Casting out demons to restore shattered lives,
repairing them from a world covered with lies.

My sisters stood up with unparalleled power,
    To make sense of a world that altered my nature.
        Protecting me from harm, they lent me their arms
so we could live in a land
where all humanity finally stands.

        All humans should know
        that a mother is the
        HEART
        of a rational life
        and a fresh new start.

My foundation was sturdy,
I had a few blokes
Slowing down the pace,
Allowing my family to
finally stand face to face.

Tower of Babble

I ponder stupidity,
but I don't understand
why people ignore me
when we should all be in one place!
        My service, most assuredly, is not my demise!
            At the end of the day, I promise you, I
            RISE.

Then the Lord said to him, "Who has made man's mouth? Who makes him mute, or deaf, or seeing, or blind?"
—Exodus 4:11

34 Gird My Loins

Truly I tell you, whatever you bind on earth will be bound in heaven, and whatever you loose on earth will be loosed in heaven.
—Matthew 18:18

To gird means to encircle, and when Jesus came to refine me, he rolled around my mind. A physical movement during the examination, in the direction of a halo, created the feeling of a band binding my head. Sinful words and thoughts from the past were released into the atmosphere and floated out into the distance, escaping my mind in preparation for receiving my promised inheritance.

I now understand what it means to gird the loins of your mind. However, it is not possible to hide anything from God. All-seeing and all-knowing, God will uncover the undiscovered. The bad words you knew you said and the ones you don't remember. The dark thoughts that came and the ones that escaped. Everything you did that wasn't God's plan, now brought to the forefront one by one; now loosed from your mind so as not to bind. Being emptied and forgiven for things long gone, things that many do while in the desert of their mind. All words, thoughts, and actions matter. They add up over time.

To gird means to prepare oneself for what lies ahead. My preparation undefined, and what's ahead—my eyes, they tried to make blind. I endeavor to prepare for what's currently out of reach. A future that predicts I'm the one who will teach. Someone looking in might think I am stuck. But the process is grueling, and I am Fort Knox.

After years of cycling from refinement to restoration, having sins washed away, I had a lucid dream in which I attended a ceremony in Heaven: Jesus took a band and placed it around my head, solidifying my mind, which resulted in much-needed peace. Christ's belt now surrounds, and my temple is secured. Now to traverse the passage to freedom, God prophesied, I would endure.

Obedience

Therefore, gird up the loins of your mind, live soberly, and set your hopes completely on the grace to be brought to you at the revelation of Jesus Christ.
—1 Peter 1:13

Band of Peace

35 Oblation of the Church

When I entered my fifties, my female cycle refused to stop—continuous for months on end. My doctor wanted me to consider removing my uterus. But for some reason, I was not comfortable doing that.   Heavenly messages were contrary.

I went to the doctor's office for an ultrasound so we could decide on the next steps. During the ultrasound, the technician found a mass in my uterus and indicated that it may be a calcification. It looked like a tiny fetus to me.   How could this be?

The technician seemed uncomfortable as she commented that it was a calcified fibroid. After the ultrasound, I was waiting in a patient room for the doctor to come to talk with me. It was taking an extremely long time;   I was sure something was wrong.

I became restless and walked out into the hall to find my doctor. I have never in my entire life seen a doctor look so terrified. He stood in the hallway with his arms and back against the wall and one foot propped up on the baseboard   —his knee bent.

Bent Knee

The look of distress on his face was like none I had ever seen. This man who had been so self-confident in my presence for the past ten years, who had seen me through the sadness and the grief of a miscarriage   —looked like he had just seen a ghost.

He was speechless and couldn't utter a word to me. A nurse handed me a form to check out. I walked past the doctor with my eyebrows raised, and in that instant, I was confident that God was taking the baby I lost back.   I was somehow going in reverse.

At least that was what my intuition screamed.

I told God many times that I wanted the baby girl I had miscarried back; I was positive I was having a daughter and prayed many times to get her back. There is nothing God can't or won't do for God's children.   So why not ask?

The next time the heavens descended on me, and the spirit started to blow through me, I jotted down some names as part of prophetic writing. Two babies were to arrive sometime in the future. A girl, Jacqueline Frances, and a boy, Jacob Israel. Would those be my children? My grandchildren?   Descendants after I die?

They can't be my children, I thought. I am too old. But, then again, so was Sarah, and God gave her a child long after her childbearing years had passed. I was hopeful that I would give birth to these babies.   Was I confused?

I missed my boys making noise, the fun we had when they were little, even the mess they made in the house. My attempt to get back to work in corporate America was a massive fail after spending years at home raising my boys.   The world had left me behind.

Corporate America had turned into a toxic pool of bodies stepping on one another to rise above. And the rules of the game were beyond my mind's grasp. Trickery was the game, and taking credit for others' work was the way.   I didn't fail. I simply refused to play.

Convinced that these babies would be mine, I came home with a pregnancy test the next day. Charles looked at me perplexed; I explained the prophetic dream I had, and that God said he was giving me my daughter back. Charles reminded me that after the miscarriage,

I asked him to fix things so we wouldn't get pregnant again.

At the time, I decided I could not bear the emotional pain of another miscarriage. Plus, Charles seemed somewhat relieved that we were not having another baby—he was in his fifties. I respected his feelings and wanted to eliminate any anxiety.

I paused for a minute, wondering how the prophecy would happen. How would I have these babies with this new hiccup? I quickly decided that if the Virgin Mary can have a baby without physical contact, why not me? I moved on   —having faith in God's words.

Several days later, my doctor called to schedule an oblation to slow my female cycle. I endured the entire oblation process without any problem other than hearing angels talking in my ears. I don't remember what was said   —but the ladies seemed excited.

My oblation procedure occurred at precisely the same time the priests' scandals came to light in Philadelphia; it was all over the news that very day. The oblation of the Catholic Church began.   A coincidence?

For me, there is no such thing as a coincidence. At least not in this lifetime. There was talk of sterilizing the priests involved so they could no longer harm children or women. What the priests had done was terrible, but sterilization seemed barbaric, mainly because the church set these men up to fail. I knew that God had no intention of priests living a lifetime of celibacy. God is love. God would never give a creature a natural drive and then require abstinence forever.
                                                 Something that contradictory is the work of the devil.

As a sweet-smelling oblation I will accept you, when I bring you from among the nations and gather you out of the lands over which you were scattered; and through you I will manifest my holiness in the sight of the nations.
—Ezekiel 20:41

36 Blessed Mother Scolds the Priests

The holy people and blameless race—it was she who delivered them from the nations that oppressed them. She entered the soul of the Lord's servant and withstood fearsome kings with signs and portents; she gave the holy ones the recompense of their labors, conducted them by wondrous road, and became a shelter for them by day and a starry flame by night. She took them across the Red Sea and brought them through the deep waters—But their enemies she overwhelmed and cast them up from the bottom and depths. Therefore, the just despoiled the wicked; and they sang, O Lord, your holy name and praised in unison your conquering hand—Because Wisdom opened the mouths of the dumb and gave ready speech to infants.
—Wisdom 10:15–21

Momma's Not Happy

One day, not long after my female oblation,
I decided to go to morning Mass at a neighboring
parish. The Holy Spirit was operating my "car," or
body, and I walked confidently into the church
and sat down in the front row.

A lady who typically attends Mass at my parish was sitting right behind me. I felt like she was there to support me for whatever reason. It was the same woman who gasped one day as she knelt next to me at Mass as if she were hearing the conversation I was having with Heaven in my mind. At any rate, I was thankful she was there because I was worried about what the Blessed Mother might do through me that day. I could feel the Blessed Mother's disgust in my bones, and Her anger was rising to a full boil inside of me. I was worried about where the Blessed Mother's anger might take me on this day but knew I had absolutely no control.

My face was scornful, with my brows furrowed during the Mass. My head nodded up and down as if I were scolding the priests presiding over the service. It appeared to me that the priests got the message based on the looks of remorse on their faces. I was positive the Blessed Mother's disgust had to do with the sexual misconduct of priests in the Catholic Church, and I agreed with Her on that. Obviously, anyone claiming to represent Jesus Christ should never commit such a heinous act on a child or anyone for that matter. Then to have it covered up was utterly despicable; I felt the revulsion in my bones and became nauseous. It was clear the Blessed Mother decided that part of the blame lay with individuals hundreds of years prior who changed the laws of the church to require priests to be only male and celibate; clearly, the church was led astray by the devil.

Before the Mass was finished, the Blessed Mother stood my body up, and we marched right out of the church; my arms were crossed, and I had a look of disgust on my face. I was thankful for the familiar voice and face of the lady behind me that day at Mass because I was far meaner and more direct when the Blessed Mother was operating my body than I was comfortable with. I aspire to be more like the Blessed Mother; She is loving but takes no shit if you mess with Her children.

**Well, maybe I am like that if I think in terms of my sons.
We may be more alike than I realize.**

"Ah, the fragrance of my son is like the fragrance of a field
   that the Lord has blessed! May God give to you
   of the dew of the heavens. And of the fertility of the earth,
   And an abundance of grain and wine. May peoples serve you,
   and nations bow down to you; Be master of your brothers,
   and may your mother's sons bow down to you.
Cursed be those who curse you and blessed be those who bless you."
—Genesis 27:27–29

Field of Lavender

Thus says the Lord: Stand in the court of the house of the Lord and speak to the inhabitants of all the cities of Judah who come to worship in the house of the Lord; whatever I command you, tell them, and hold nothing back. Perhaps they will listen and turn, all of them from their evil way, so that I may repent of the evil I plan to inflict upon them for their evil deeds.
—Jeremiah 26:2-3

Dreams

As purification in heaven continued for my impending union with Jesus, my dreams became more vivid and compelling. It was like going from playing Atari games to playing Xbox games. The dreams were not of human origin or like anything I had experienced before. In the first dream, I was in a bedroom dancing with a magnificent male angel. He was tall, handsome, and muscular, wearing a long gown with a sash over it. We danced, he romanced me, I was enticed, and then he left.

In the next dream there was another gorgeous male angel with a long gown, and he danced with me and romanced me in a lustful way. It was exhilarating. I felt like I must be in heaven because the dreams were inconceivable but magnificent. Then the second angel informed me that I could be with him three nights a week and with the first angel three nights a week, and one night I would be alone.

I started to panic and yelled, "Jesus, where are you? You said you would never leave me or abandon me." Jesus showed up instantly and took me in his arms and held me. He said, "I am here just like I told you I would be, my love. Just call for me if you are not sure about something, or if you are scared, and I will be there as promised." I knew seven days and nights a week with Jesus is better than six evenings of romance with two different angels, only to end up alone; I only wanted Jesus. We danced and he held me tight—great peace and calmness came over me; I was safe.

119

I thought about this dream for days to come and knew I was
getting ready to face the pain at my core. Jesus had been massaging my
flaws and aches out gently for years now. It was time for the significant issues
to surface and be dealt with. My soul needed to be healed so I could get on with
doing the work God sent me here to do. I wanted this to happen much
faster, but clearly, it was not going to.

As the issues came to the surface, I began to "vomit" my
pent-up emotions and feelings. Not something I wanted to do; I
liked hiding behind my concrete wall and going along pretending I
was okay. It seemed to make the outside world happy. These problems
were not ones I wanted to face or share with anybody, ever. But the
past is somehow lingering right into my present. And I am being
forced to look at myself in the mirror. I guess I must face
my truth sometime.

Dream

The following night, I had another vivid dream: I am walking in a parking garage with Buck
and a woman I believe to be an angel. Buck and the angel walk up the stairs, and I take the elevator
to meet Buck after lying on the floor of the elevator for some reason. I wake up, get up off the floor,
and hit two buttons to go up. I stop on one floor but don't get off the elevator. I stay on and go all
the way to the top. When I get there, the angel is gone. It is just Buck waiting for me.

Buck and I walk to an old hotel that has a restaurant, and we sit down for dinner on the
outdoor patio. I have a vivid picture of the estate; I could see it so clearly, I felt like I was physically
there. As we walk into the hotel, there is a restaurant on the left with ten to fifteen tables full of
dinner guests eating. A plethora of antiques is hanging from the walls and ceiling to decorate the
restaurant. On the right, there are built-in bookshelves, floor to ceiling, along the entire wall. The
shelves are full of books and knickknacks.

But we don't stay in the main restaurant. We follow the hostess past the bookshelves and through a narrow corridor. The bookshelves are still on our right, and on the left are two doors. The first door, I find out later, goes to the basement, and then there is a little wall with a small table for two, and then a door to the bathroom. As we continue past, we go through a door that leads to the outdoor dining room. We sit at a table right outside the door next to the outdoor grill. We are under a pergola covered in vines.

We order food and drink, talk, and catch up for hours. I start crying and fill a cloth napkin with tears until it's soaked. I'm not sure why I'm crying, to be honest. I see Buck vividly just as if I were with him on Earth, but I'm not sure what he did or said to make me cry. Taking the napkin with me, I get up to go to the bathroom but instead sit at the table next to the bathroom to talk to someone. Who? I don't know. I wring out the tears from the napkin on the floor under the table, creating a large puddle. The waitress comes over and is annoyed with me. I tell her tears evaporate—take a chill pill. I get up to go look for something to clean it up with. I decide to go downstairs to look for a bucket and mop. As I head down the stairs, I notice the basement is full of various kinds of lettuces and other greens. How bizarre, I think to myself. I never get to the bottom of the staircase because some man calls out to me from upstairs. I go back up the stairs, and a floating piece of greenery tries to follow me. I bat it down and close the door behind me.

The main restaurant is to my right, and people are saying they are not sure they like the wood used for the hardwood floors. What does the kind of wood have to do with the food? I ignore them and walk back toward the table to rejoin Buck. On the way there, I dust off a ledge and part of the grill with my motorcycle glove. Again, bizarre. Buck and I get our leftovers and go up to our room. We are lying in bed, my head is on his chest, and the TV is on. We talk for a while, and Buck says something about his mom. I can't remember what he said about her. Then he says, "Let's read the book you wrote." I say, "You read it." Buck says, "No, let's do it together because you must fill in the blank spaces." We sit up, and he has a stack of five or so books, and some are stuffed between pages of others to mark places as if he had been reading them. Buck reads some, then hands me the stack, saying, "You must fill all those blank spaces with the words of your poems and your fearless life." He adds, "Learn to ride the motorcycle. Live fearlessly."

I wake up from my dream and cry—I mean, I sob uncontrollably, and I don't entirely understand why.

I get up, go to the bathroom, and then get back in bed and go to Jesus in the upper room in my mind. Jesus and I are sitting on two chairs that face one another, and I lay my head on his lap and cry while he rubs my back.

I lie awake in my bed on earth that morning and heard the angels singing. It was all men for some reason, but beautiful. I listened a long time, speculating on where the women angels had gone and then drift back to sleep.

When I was waking later that morning, I had a vision in which I was riding a motorcycle and fell. My shoulder and the right side of my head hit the pavement; my neck became elongated. As I woke, I felt the base of my head on the right side, beating as if blood was flowing through it, and it had a heartbeat. I saw my right hand was gone and replaced with a hook. I panicked for a second, then saw Jesus's hand with the hole and realized I was attached to his hand with my hook. I was permanently tethered to Jesus by love. Then the following words came into my mind:

"What I say to you, I say to all."

I knew the minute I woke the morning after this dream that I was going to have to call Buck. The dream was so real, and as hard as I had tried over the years to block him from my mind, it seems as if my affection for him was expanding exponentially across the universe, and I had no power to stop it. This must be part of the purging process I am going through, I thought. For sure, if I were in control, I would never face these feelings but would take them to my grave.

There is nowhere to hide from God;
I knew that. I must face this soon.

Therefore, thus says the Lord God: See, I am laying a stone in Zion, a stone that has been tested, A precious cornerstone as a sure foundation; whoever puts faith in it will not waver. I will make judgment a measuring line, and justice a level.—Hail shall sweep away the refuge of lies, and waters shall flood the hiding place. Your covenant with death shall be canceled and your pact with Sheol shall not stand. When the raging flood passes through, you shall be beaten down by it. Whenever it passes, it shall seize you; morning after morning it shall pass, by day and by night. Sheer terror to impart the message!
—Isaiah 28:16–19

Hook

38 Lobbies Connected

Complete my joy by being of the same mind, with the same love, united in heart, thinking one thing.
—Philippians 2:2

The morning after the dream, I sat in my bed for a long time overwhelmed by how palpable the dream was. Why was I having such vivid dreams about a boy of my youth after all these years? My mind wandered back to my college days when Buck and I were at the University of Pittsburgh; I was stuck in an elevator on the first day of our freshman year. I lived in the dorm called Tower B, and Buck lived in Tower C; our lobbies connected.

I was coming down in the elevator from the twenty-first floor to meet Buck in the lobby, and we were going out to some parties. The elevator was overloaded with freshmen, and it started to free-fall, then stopped suddenly and began to fly back up. Everyone was screaming. When we reached the top, the elevator started falling again, and we ended up stuck underground for over an hour. There were so many students crammed into the elevator that it was hard to breathe. We took turns standing up and then sitting down on the elevator floor so we could get air—horrendous! Buck waited in the lobby for me until the rescue team pulled me and the others out from the basement. I was dripping with sweat by the time we went out that night, but Buck never left; he waited for me.

College was a sublime time for us. We had friends, fun, and did some studying, too. Buck and I would hang out in the dorms freshman year, then in subsequent years in our apartments listening to music and playing games. Buck was into Led Zeppelin, and I loved Prince; we would listen to music and play backgammon or cards.

I recently listened to many of those songs again and thought about how the lyrics blend my past with my present, right through to the future I see in my dreams.

A Prince?

I dented my little red convertible.
Because I was trying to have fun.
I guess I should slow down.
        It was 1999 when the shock in my spine
        drove me underground. My emotions smoldered.
            My life went completely astray.

I wanted to dance, but my balance was lost;
When revelation knocked, I answered the door.
        Not enough thought—left pieces scattered.
            I take the elevator when a stairway is needed.

Whatever I ask, my Father answers;
Not always the one that I want.
The words that I read often mislead,
        but eventually, I conjure a meaning.
        I confirm my direction by testing spirits;
            Evil lurks around the next corner.

My smoke rings improve with the dip in my mood.
        As I sit in the west, facing demons and unrest,
            I wonder if there are any tears of regret.

The wash and spin cycles disclose my secrets.
As I'm drawn by the Spirit to the light of a new day,
        May I enter the kingdom cleansed.
        I have determined my path—my decision is rock solid.
            I refuse to change direction.

The light that I'm under illuminates truths undiscovered.
        The Spirit's the answer to a unified whole,
            All become one and one become all

The glory of God's golden ages.

The summer between our freshman and sophomore years of college, Buck and I were home in Erie, Pennsylvania, and my parents were hosting a family Fourth of July cookout. Buck and my brother-in-law, Todd, were playing Frisbee in our backyard, which was densely populated with trees, when Buck's face met a tree, crushing his beautiful left cheekbone like a potato chip. He was in severe pain and would end up needing surgery to repair his face. My dad yelled at me just after the accident to stay back; he didn't want me to see how badly injured Buck was. I refused and ran right to Buck's side. That was the day my mom declared, "This is the one she loves."

Recently, I dug out a picture taken shortly after the surgery Buck underwent to repair his face. It dawned on me that the way Buck and I are positioned in the picture resembles the Delphic Sibyl on the ceiling of the Sistine Chapel—the way the man's head is just behind the woman's head. My mind often connects items in history with memories of Buck and me, right through to prophetic visions and dreams I have of the future. I didn't know precisely how or why this was happening, but it was, and there were way too many connections for it to be random. My life was being flawlessly pieced together through time and space.

As I mentioned earlier, "our song" when Buck and I were kids was "I Can't Hold Back" by Survivor. My life is falling right in line with the lyrics of this song from my youth:

My eyes see a universal story that others apparently cannot. The desire Buck and I felt for one another was robust during our youth, but it has become clear that the Passion of Christ was our job to fulfill even before we were born. My spine always trembled at the touch of his hand, and now I hear his thoughts in my head daily. All these concepts are embedded in the song's lyrics.

Buck broke up with me once during our freshman year of college, and then we were solid until senior year. Toward the end of our senior year, he decided again that he wanted to date other people and we parted ways. It was around that time that my parrot flew out the bedroom window of his apartment; Buck lost my bird, and my heart was crushed once again. I was finally determined to move on. I had been dumped one too many times by Buck and decided I was not going to wait around any longer. I began dating.

History Repeats

Delphic Sybil

Buck and I were separated for a couple of months before I started dating. The boy I was dating and I had plans to go out on the evening of Buck's birthday. Buck must have been having second thoughts about letting me go because he called me on his birthday to see if I would go out and celebrate with him. I told him, not a chance—I had a date. I wasn't particularly interested in the new boy I was dating, but it was a diversion from dwelling on a relationship that caused me nothing but heartache and pain. I was determined to move on with my life. I was done feeling second rate. I was done being with someone who always seemed to be looking for someone else.

Well, Buck decided to show up at the bar he knew I frequented and saw me sitting with my date. Buck got very upset and slammed a bottle on the bar right in front of me, covering me and my date with beer, then stormed out of the bar and kicked a mailbox on the sidewalk. The police arrested Buck for that act and hauled him off to jail; apparently, kicking a mailbox is a federal offense. I had no idea until weeks later what had happened to him. But that was pretty much the end of our relationship. Buck took his school ring out of the plaque he'd made for me that said, "I CAN'T HOLD BACK" AMY I LOVE YOU!, and left me with an empty space.

Our union was broken; the mailbox was dented.

Our senior year of college quickly came to an end, and I landed a job in Philadelphia while Buck ended up going home to finish college classes. His trip to jail caused him to miss some tests and not complete the courses he needed to graduate.

I would see Buck one more time about seven months later at Christmastime when I went home to visit my dad. Buck and I met at a bar, had a couple of drinks, and then went to his sister's apartment and caught up while sitting in her jet tub. We parted ways that night, and I hadn't talked to Buck since. Not that I hadn't thought about him or tried to find him over the past twenty-eight years, because I had. Many times, but with no success.

Mailbox

39 Reunion After Twenty-Eight Years

But if you do not dispossess the inhabitants of the land before you, those whom you allow to remain will become barbs in your eyes and thorns in your sides, and they will harass you in the land where you live, and I will treat you as I had intended to treat them.
—Numbers 33:55-56

Now that I had left Charles and was in my own apartment, it seemed like a good time to try to find Buck and hopefully get beyond this thorn in my side that was preventing me from transforming into what God was calling me to be.

I felt ridiculous seeking out my college boyfriend all these years later, but I did. I searched online and discovered that he was married and living about four hours from me in Atlanta. I entered his name and phone number into my cell phone and decided to think about what I was going to say before calling.

Eventually, I punched in the number and got his voicemail. My message went something like this: "Hi Buck, this is Amy Jean, just calling to catch up with you. I know it has been a while, but I would love to hear how you are doing, old friend." Buck returned the call a couple of days later.

When I saw his name on my cell as it rang, I took a deep breath ... then I answered the call. Buck's voice sounded the same as I remembered it from when we were kids. We talked briefly and shared the quick and positive versions of our lives. Buck married a couple of years after I had, and he and his wife had a son and daughter—a happy and prosperous life. I shared the positive part of my story about Charles and our three sons.

Interestingly, I mentioned to Buck that it had been three decades since we had spoken, and he quickly corrected me, saying it had been twenty-eight years. I knew exactly how long it had been myself but wanted to sound casual. The conversation was pleasant, but after we hung up, thoughts of our past together began to harass my mind daily. The thorn I was trying to extricate from my life was refusing to be tweezed out.

A month later, I decided to go to Atlanta for a Home Builders Association meeting. The franchisor of my cleaning company wanted me to open a franchise in Atlanta, but I had been avoiding looking into it. I was too busy running my operations in the Charlotte and Raleigh markets already. But with Buck conveniently living in the area, I decided to evaluate the opportunity. I had no intention of opening a franchise there; my trip to Atlanta was primarily to see Buck in hopes of getting him out of my head once and for all.

Buck eventually agreed to meet me after work one day. We met at a sports bar not far from my Atlanta hotel. I was surprisingly calm about the meeting, and in hindsight, I'm quite sure the spirit was flowing through me that day because I didn't feel entirely "present" when I was with him. I felt like I was on a mission to share my story with Buck, rid my mind of my unhealthy attachment to him, and get on with God's plan for me—extract the thorn! Here's how our reunion went:

I walk up to the door of the restaurant, and
> Buck steps out and opens the door for me as if he senses my arrival.
>> Quite odd since there is no window that he can see me through.
>>> Maybe Buck is psychic like me?
>>> We hug briefly.

Buck says, "You have aged gracefully."
> I say, "Thank you. It's so nice to see you after all these years: twenty-eight, I believe."
>> Buck grins and holds the door for me as we enter the restaurant.

He looks worn out—bags under his eyes, some extra weight, and a receding hairline.
> This should help me move past the stupid youthful crush I have on him.
>> Not that I can talk. I have wrinkles, bags under my eyes, and graying hair.

Maybe Buck is just being nice in saying that I have aged gracefully.

High Top Table

We sit down at a high-top table across from the bar. Buck is already drinking a Guinness. Maybe he is nervous. I order a glass of wine and ask Buck for the CliffsNotes version of his life and an update on his family. I realize his wife is probably at home waiting for him, and I feel uncomfortable tying up her husband for the entire evening. Buck tells me about his family, career, frequent relocations, and hobbies. Then he fills me in on his eight brothers and sisters, and his parents. I remember all his siblings' names, and he is impressed.

Buck randomly points out that my sister and her husband are still married. How odd. Why is he telling me that? I know my sister and her husband are married. Was Buck implying that I should stay with my husband? I don't even mention to him that I had left Charles. But somehow, I feel like he is telling me to go back to Charles. I let the thought pass and focus on the rest of Buck's story about his life and family. Buck's life is happy and prosperous, and all his family members are doing well. I get a warm feeling inside for him and am sincerely glad he has enjoyed such a beautiful life up to this point.

40 Understood

"Behold, my eye has seen all this, my ear has heard and understood it. What you know, I also know; I am not inferior to you."
—Job 13:1–2

After twenty-eight years,
I was again oddly comfortable in Buck's presence.
I sat at the high-top bar table and told him my entire life story since we had parted.
Literally everything, including my walk with Jesus Christ,
the bad decisions I had made when I went back to work,
the issues with my neighbors in Ohio,
all the dumb stuff I had done in my life,
and all my great joys.

Buck believed every word I said. The first person so far who literally believed me without question. I could see in Buck's eyes that he had no doubts either. Damn, I thought to myself, at this moment, I feel like I am home somehow. A weight lifted from my shoulders. I was not crazy in Buck's presence, but sane, understood, and accepted.

How perplexing to feel so close and comfortable with someone who was essentially now a stranger after twenty-eight years of separation. The feeling was disarming and arming at the same time. The polarity of my feelings confounded me; a piece of me wanted to melt into his arms and cry to release years of pent-up emotions, and another piece felt like I was sitting with a virtual stranger and needed to put my guard up to prevent further injury and damage to my brokenness.

A feeling of panic swept over me, knowing that Buck was happily married. I didn't want to feel so comfortable with him, and there was no way I would accept being heartbroken for eternity; I would retrain my brain, and eventually, my heart. I calmed myself by deciding that I was no longer sexually attracted to Buck, so removing him from my thoughts would not be a problem. Maybe he would just be an old friend now, someone I could talk to. That is what I told myself. We talked for maybe three hours and then parted ways with a brief hug outside the bar.

On my drive back to Charlotte the next day, I was thinking back over the previous four years trapped in heaven's virtual prison, remembering how Buck kept coming to the surface every time I would go through a spin cycle in the refiner's fire while the Spirit was flowing through me. For example, I kept seeing a hairband and then a hairclip. Buck always liked my hair long, and I would frequently put it up in a hairband to make a ponytail. Charles preferred my hair shorter and curly with just a clip on one side. I sensed the angels in heaven were trying to get me to think about this conflict rooted deep in my heart, forcing me into a resolution. I would hear the song "Meet Virginia," by Train, on the radio and the lyrics about Virginia not wanting to be the queen and how she would pull her hair back. It would make me think that maybe I didn't want to wear a hairclip or be a queen. A hairband suits me better.

Another thing that kept surfacing in my mind was that Buck always hated me putting my cold feet on his when we were in bed together, but Charles never minded me warming my feet with his. At least, until the last couple of years. More recently, sometimes Charles was fine with me putting my cold feet on him, and other times he would pull away. Was I being lured into thinking about Buck by these new odd behaviors on Charles's part? Another thing that was off was that sometimes Charles's eyes looked blue and other times they were brown. And why all of the sudden did Charles drink Guinness? That is the beer Buck was drinking when I met him in Atlanta. I suspected that I was supposed to understand that sometimes Buck was ghosting me through Charles based on information I had gathered from the universe through song lyrics on the radio. I was collecting evidence through various mediums that my life had been reduced to a game somehow. I had no intention of playing an idiotic game. My mind couldn't grasp why I would play a game of human life—why were we participating in the game at all? I wanted to live a life where I could talk to the person I was looking at. I no longer understood where I was or what was being done to me.

Why am I facing childhood conflicts so many years later? Is this a part of the game that is being played with my life? Why are they working so hard to figure me out from afar instead of just coming to me and asking me questions directly?

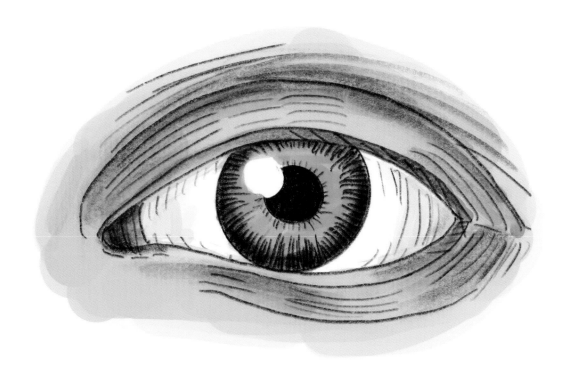

SEE

41 Seven Husbands?

On that day some Sadducees came to Jesus and questioned Him, asking, "Teacher, Moses said, 'If a man dies having no children, his brother as next of kin shall marry his wife, and raise up children for his brother.' Now there were seven brothers with us; and the first married and died, and having no children left his wife to his brother; so also, the second, and the third, down to the seventh. Last of all, the woman died. In the resurrection, therefore, whose wife of the seven will she be? For they all had married her." But Jesus answered and said to them, "You are mistaken, not understanding the Scriptures nor the power of God. For in the resurrection they neither marry nor are given in marriage but are like angels in heaven. But regarding the resurrection of the dead, have you not read what was spoken to you by God: 'I am the God of Abraham, and the God of Isaac, and the God of Jacob'? He is not the God of the dead but of the living." When the crowds heard this, they were astonished at His teaching.
—Matthew 22:23–33

When I read this Scripture and gained an understanding of God's message to me,
       I am quite sure my
            head began to
                 s
                     p
                i
              n
              and not the desired
          s
        p
         i
          n
             of the halo that I believed was sitting on my head, but the
evil kind like in the movie The Exorcist, where your head turns in two directions at the same time you are vomiting.

Suddenly I had a new understanding of what God was telling me. I flashed back instantly to a "spin" I had in the fire a couple of years back when I rattled off the name of every man I had united with during my "lost" days between my relationships with Buck and my relationship with Charles. Sure enough, there were five men, bringing the total to seven as the number of men my flesh met with. And in God's eyes, that would be a total of seven husbands.

In an attempt to rid myself of my heartache after Buck tossed me aside, I searched for a replacement, but to no avail. I am not proud of my activity during my lost days and considered leaving sins too personal to remain between the lines rather than have them printed for eternity. But the truth is that I am a disciple of Jesus Christ, and what kind of a disciple tells only part of their story that raises Him up? Not me. Jesus sacrificed for me, so I, in turn, can suffer whatever consequences may come my way for baring all on his behalf. My life was fitting right with the Bible stories daily. And today:

A wife in God's eyes with seven husbands.

Mary Magdalene had seven demons. Maybe these men were the demons I was being cleansed of. Not that they were bad men, but perhaps I had to be cleansed of my sin related to these men before my union with Jesus. A rewind of sorts to purify me so I would be "whole" before I was with Jesus.

Demons

42 My Cup Set Aside

The cup of the Lord
Awake, awake!
Arise, O Jerusalem,
You who drank at the Lord's hand the cup of his wrath;
Who drained to the dregs? The bowl of staggering
She has no one to grasp her by the hand,
Of all the sons she bore!–She has no one to grasp her by the hand,
Of all the sons she reared!–Your misfortunes are double;
Who is there to condole with you?
Desolation and destruction, famine and sword! Who is there to comfort you?
Your sons lie helpless, At every street corner like antelopes in a net.
They are filled with the wrath of the Lord, the rebuke of your God
But now, hear this, O afflicted one, Drunk, but not with wine
Thus, says the Lord your master, your God who defends his people:
See I am taking from your hand the cup of staggering;
The bowl of my wrath, you shall no longer drink,
I will put it into the hands of your tormentors,
Those who ordered you to bow down, that they might walk over you,
While you offered your back like the ground,
Like the street for them to walk on.
—Isaiah 51:17–23

Chalice

At Mass three days before Easter on March 29, 2018, when I entered the upper room of my mind and went to sit at the banquet table, Jesus pulled out the chair to his right so I could sit next to him. When it was time to hold up my chalice and drink the wine, Jesus put his hand on the base of the chalice so that I couldn't pick it up, and he handed me his chalice to drink from.

Would I no longer continue to suffer?
Was this the end of carrying my cross?

Or was it just a break in my purification?

I felt sick to my stomach over the extent of my sins at this point in the process, but Jesus was shining so brightly on my imperfections that I couldn't see them being washed away. If Jesus could accept me and take me back, then I guess,

Jesus will take anyone back.

Who is there like you, the God who removes guilt and pardons sin for the remnant of his inheritance; Who does not persist in anger forever, but delights rather in clemency, and will again, have compassion on us, treading underfoot our guilt? You will show faithfulness to Jacob, and grace to Abraham, as you have sworn to our fathers from days old.
—Micah 7:18–20

By April 2018, I decided to move back home. Charles called me, teary-eyed, and said he missed me terribly. I felt like I had completed the necessary task of facing Buck and resolved my conflicting feelings toward him. Not only was Buck happily married and unavailable, but I decided I was not physically attracted to him any longer; this issue had been put to bed. I was being resurrected and repaired, and while I knew God was trying to tell me how things would be for me upon completion, I didn't know what that was. I would go back home to Charles; it was a safe harbor to rest.

During my three months in the apartment, my sons were surprisingly supportive of me. All three boys clearly knew something extraordinary had been going on with me for years; they were "taken from me" long ago. Our relationship had become like every relationship in my life— synthetic, orchestrated, contrived. I was aware that they knew I was experiencing Heaven, that they believed me, and possibly that they knew precisely who I was. Maybe even better than I knew myself. But they would not say so. Why not? I assumed it was part of my exile.

If my boys had been having natural interactions with me, they would have been pissed off that I had left their father. No question about it. Particularly Benjamin; he never held back his emotions when he encountered things that mattered. I often wished I was as good at telling people exactly what I thought. But I wasn't.

Since my virtual lockup, the boys called Charles more than me to talk, which I became accustomed to. They relied on me when they were younger, but once they hit their teens, they preferred to talk to their father. Young men at their age typically model themselves after their fathers. Especially if they have a good father. And my boys have a great father. It made sense that I would return home to Charles and continue with the life we were enjoying together. My three sons seemed happy about our reunion, and the anxiety I was feeling over making my sons uncomfortable lifted. I was determined to push Buck gradually out of my thoughts as I had decades ago.

I texted Buck a time or two over the next few months, and he texted back, and then we didn't communicate at all for several months. We had caught up, and now we were moving on. I decided I would text Buck on Christmas Day and his birthday as any old friend might do. I didn't want to disturb his life. I wanted to focus on reuniting my family.

Family Reunion

43 Fly Lessons

Dream

I sit in the basement looking at the TV screen holding a remote, playing an addictive video game in which I am flying my body like an airplane. I sit for hours going in circles above the clouds, over the mountains, through valleys, and across large bodies of water. I finally realize I am wasting my time pretending to live rather than getting out and living free.

I get up and climb the stairs to the first floor of my house and grab my car keys. The keys to the car my dad built for me when I was a kid. We brought the car home on a flatbed truck in pieces. My dad constructed it piece by piece over many months, making sure it was perfect and building confidence that he, and only he, would know how to repair it to perfection. Once Dad had the engine running and was positive that all the parts were in working order, we started examining colors for the paint job. After careful consideration, we narrowed it down to two shades: either candy-apple red or fire-engine red. I made the final choice of candy-apple red. I walk down the hallway and out the front door, keys in hand, and get into my Triumph Spitfire convertible.

I drive over to my husband's gym to take charge of my life. I was done sitting around waiting for something to happen, done looking at screens. I was ready to take charge and live my life large—completely fearless. My husband's gym is the largest gym in the world; you can do everything from fly fishing to basketball to flying an open-air, self-propelled plane. I walk in the front door and past the guards. They know me there since it's my husband's gym and I go frequently; I have priority access. To the right is a huge basketball court, but it is empty. To the left are two enormous rooms for fly fishing. A few fishermen called out to me asking if I wanted to fish, but I say no; I would rather fly.

I walked past the lady at the center counter and tell her I am going to head up to see my husband and talk about taking a flight. She indicates that he is not there now. I tell her I will go up and wait. I crawl under the concrete ledge to get to the staircase and climb the stairs to the tower room. When I entered the tower room, it is empty. I look around at the flight suits and decide, "I can do this." I put the self-propelled suit on and step out onto the launchpad. After a few minutes of debating with myself about whether I should try to fly on my own, I decide to go for it. I take a leap of faith and begin to free-fall. I panic and start to pedal and flap the wings. The plane goes in one circle and then peters out. I land in the field behind my husband's gym, breaking the right wingtip. Several workers from the gym come running out to see if I am okay. They help me get the self-propelled plane back into the gym.

The workers start telling me that my husband is upset. I start heading back to climb the stairs again, and they are yelling out to me that I'd better not go back up because my husband is there and they are worried he is mad. I turn briefly and say, "You don't know my husband, do you? We always find each other and make up by the end of the day."

I crawl under the concrete slab and back up the steps to the tower. I tell my husband what happened, and he gives me a kiss. He shows me how to use the self-propelled plane and proceeds to fix the right wing so I can give it another try. He also gives me pointers on how to use the wings. Then he walks me out to the edge, where he stands right behind me shouting words of encouragement. With His words of encouragement and protection in my mind, I gain new confidence beyond what I had felt before.

I am pedaling hard and at the same time gracefully moving the broad wings with their massive span, allowing me to fly. Before I know it, I am soaring out around the universe with my husband somehow holding onto me from afar to make sure I won't fall this time. I pedal a pattern that leads me straight up to the top of the sky. I am at the top of what looks like a giant tidal wave in the sky. I split into four and spread north, south, east, and west like a firework. When I come back together and circle back to the gym, I realize that I am the cleansed and beautiful woman at the top of the tidal wave that I had seen in my dream the night before.

The flight was a little scary, but I was fearless and amazing. I can hear the crowd on the ground cheering me on: "Whoa, She's killing it; She can fly after all!" And then as I soar back toward my husband, I hear him shouting, "Now that's my Wife—fearless, flying right up to the top where She belongs."

See what great love the Father has lavished on us, that we should be called children of God! And that is what we are!
—1 John 3:1

Wings

44 Walking on Water

When evening came, his disciples went down to the lake, where they got into a boat and set off across the lake for Capernaum. By now it was dark, and Jesus had not yet joined them. A strong wind was blowing, and the waters grew rough. When they had rowed about three or four miles, they saw Jesus approaching the boat, walking on the water; and they were frightened. But he said to them, "It is I; don't be afraid." Then they were willing to take him into the boat, and immediately the boat reached the shore where they were heading.
—John 6:16-21

Three months passed with no communication between Buck and me. Life was back to "normal," if you want to call it that. My husband Charles, the boys, and I went to a cabin in Maine that we rent every summer for a week. Our best friends from Pennsylvania and their children were there with us. There were seventeen of us staying in a little cabin with one bathroom. It was remote and dirty, with no internet or TV, and yet the best vacation every year for the past sixteen years. We swim, fish, kayak, paddleboard, hike, play volleyball, read, sit around the campfire, overeat, and drink way too much, which results in laughter and childish behavior—a total blast. This year, with my newfound ability to have my mind in Heaven and my body on Earth in tandem, something incredible happened to me:

I awake one morning with the sun's rays just starting to crest over the edge of the skylight above me. I stretch my arms up and roll on my side to grab my cell phone off the nightstand. It is 6:00 a.m. My feet hit the wood planks of the flooring, and I pull on my swimsuit, shuffle into my flip-flops, and head down the creaky steps of the cabin to discover I am, once again, the only person up at this early hour.

Yes! I proclaim as I grab a cup of coffee and head quickly down to the beach area. The lake at Tricky Pond is a sheet of glass, utterly untouched by the new day. The sun is just cresting over the tall pines on the other side of the lake; the campers are not yet awake.

143

I step onto my paddleboard, and as I place the paddle in the water on one side to propel myself forward, I put the very first ripple on the glassy surface—me, the source of the first movement on the pond. I lift the paddle out of the water and do the same on the other side of my board. Now ripples spread across the pond in two directions. The untouched surface of the lake has been broken, and the new day has begun. I am the originator of the day on the lake.

I pause briefly to look back at the cabin. Still not a stir; sixteen adults are sleeping safe and sound. The early morning is entirely mine. As I paddle away from the cabin, I look down through the crystal-clear lake, where rocks, aged logs, and fish can be seen on the bottom. Then I look up and see three adult and three baby loons having what looks like a morning meeting. I continue paddling down the lake to two little islands at the other end.

Walking on Water

Reaching the water between the two islands, I sit down cross-legged on my paddleboard, close my eyes, and go to the upper room of my mind to meditate. Maybe an hour passes, and I open my eyes, then stand up to continue my paddle around the lake. As I begin to paddle, I am at least forty feet above the trees looking down on the lake, and yet my feet are still on the paddleboard. The view is incredible; I am walking on water with my head inexplicably soaring above while my feet are on the paddleboard gliding across the lake. After maybe ten minutes, my head drifts back to earth. My Divine transformation is most definitely occurring.

Later that same day, I received a text from Buck with a picture of a car just like the Triumph Spitfire my dad built me when I was sixteen. Buck is driving the car with his son in the passenger seat. We texted back and forth a few times that day reminiscing about the car. Buck asked questions about what year and color the car was.

Ugh, I think to myself.
I worked hard to put Buck out of my mind.
What is he doing?

Buck reminded me that my car was a hybrid of two different model years that my Dad combined to build it and that we painted it candy-apple red. Was he being helpful by attempting to bring smothered memories to the surface as so many people from my past have done in recent years?

Or is Buck out there thinking about me?

45 God's Divine Army

The seventy returned with joy, saying, "Lord, even the demons are subject to us in Your name." And He said to them, "I was watching Satan fall from heaven like lightning. Behold, I have given you authority to tread on serpents and scorpions, and over all the power of the enemy, and nothing will injure you. Nevertheless, do not rejoice in this, that the spirits are subject to you, but rejoice that your names are recorded in heaven."
—Luke 10:17–20

Spirits Intervene on My Behalf

I was trying hard to live in the moment and be of good cheer like Saint Paul, knowing that 2020 would be the end of seven years of suffering and hopefully the end of my exile from humanity. I was ready to have natural conversations and interactions with my family and friends. Isolation and loneliness had become my norm, and I was comfortable on my own, but my life was starting to feel pointless. What good was it to see and know Heavenly things if nobody will listen to what I have to say or take me seriously? I was trying to live moment to moment to grab joy each day, and on most days, I was doing that by myself. I was dancing on my own around my family room, laughing at the insanity of my life when I wasn't crying, playing with my dogs, and from time to time enjoying moments with my sons despite knowing we were not being completely genuine with one another. They knew I was the fulfillment of the prophet Isaiah, Lady Zion, but refused to confirm it.

The reality that transpired in my mind was the only place where I received any confirmation of my beliefs. It seemed like my prayers were being answered daily. One day at morning Mass, the Spirit spoke right through me. Instead of saying the words "Lord be with my Spirit," I uttered, "Lord be with my sin." I was startled when I realized what had just come out of my mouth. The Spirit was leading me back to ask for additional cleansing so I could move forward on my journey. I was thankful for the Spirit's help as I was growing incredibly weary on what felt like a never-ending journey.

I decided to follow the Spirit's lead, and I knelt, closed my eyes, and entered the upper room in my mind. I confessed any remaining sins I could think of to Jesus and asked him if he forgave me. Jesus smiled gently and said, "Of course I do. Do you forgive you?" The Spirit was guiding me to turn over all of my impurities to the Lord. I realized that if Jesus Christ could forgive me, then most assuredly, I should be able to forgive myself. For the rest of that day, I felt a freedom that I don't experience every day. Each moment felt like Heaven.

A few days after that, I headed up to Highlands, North Carolina, to get away for the weekend. I wanted some time to myself to meditate, write, and think. The road up to the mountains was winding and rain trickled across the windshield the entire trip, which was farther away than I realized.

As I got closer to my hotel, I sensed it was going to be my time of the month that the Spirit would flow through me. I had somehow moved from having a female cycle to a monthly movement of the Spirit flowing through me instead. I was unsure at this point which I preferred. But the more I understood about what was happening when heaven was flowing through me, the more interesting my new monthly event became.

When I arrived in Highlands, I decided to check out the town, stroll through the shops, and get a bite to eat. I noticed immediately as I walked through town that several things seemed "off." First, the weather was odd. It was shifting quickly from sunny and warm, with an atmosphere charged with new life, to overcast and subdued, with an eerie stillness that was unsettling. Weather can be unpredictable, but the rapid shift between the weather patterns was unnatural—unlike any weather pattern I had ever experienced. Then as I looked at the families around me, all the children were girls. Not a single young boy anywhere, and the town was full of people walking around, shopping, and eating at the outdoor tables.

I decided to stop at a restaurant at the top of the little town to grab dinner before heading to my hotel for the evening. The hostess took my name and motioned to benches out front where I could wait until my table was ready. I walked past a mother with three young girls sitting on one of the benches with an older woman who looked to be the grandmother. The older woman looked directly at me and said, "We thought pigs would fly before we would see you down here." I quizzically raised my eyebrows, then turned around to look behind me, thinking maybe she was talking to someone else. There was nobody there. I turned back toward the woman, and her daughter looked right at me and said, "There are a lot of good people here, you know. It is so good of you to come."

At that moment, I realized that while I walked around the town in awe of the shifting weather patterns, I was repeatedly reciting in my head the mantra that I had made up for Jesus to scare demons away: "Begone evil spirits, do you not know who I am? I am the beloved servant of Jesus Christ, his sister, his bride, Lady Zion, and the one predicted by the prophet Isaiah. Begone, evil spirits, or I will summon my husband." I was casting out demons for Jesus without knowing it, which really means that Jesus was casting out demons and I was the vessel he was flowing through. Where exactly was I? I wasn't sure what dimension or realm I was in, but I was most definitely not "driving my own body."

When Pigs Fly

Anyway, I was shown to a table along one side of the restaurant and ordered some food and a glass of wine. While I was thinking about the work I was doing for Jesus, a woman walked up with a little pig on a leash! No kidding—a pig on a leash. When pigs fly—a rarity if it occurs at all.

I went back to my hotel and decided to get into the hot tub outside to unwind. Casting out demons, not knowing what you are doing until it is all over, is stressful. I put my swimsuit on and headed down the steps at the end of the hall. I sat alone in the hot tub, stargazing as I attempted to quiet my mind. After a nice soak, I dried off and decided to head back to my room. I went back in the same door I exited the hotel from and walked up the staircase to the second floor where my room was, but somehow, I came out at the opposite end of the hotel! How? I have no clue!

Must be part of my ride—it's wild!

The next morning, I stopped at some waterfalls before heading back to Charlotte. Bridal Veil Falls just had a little trickle of water flowing, but Dry Falls was bountiful and gorgeous. Everything seemed to be exactly the opposite of what I was expecting.

Dry Falls

46 Feed the Homeless

Instructions from Heaven were flowing to me freely and quickly now. I was tuned in to what Jesus was telling me, and this made life somewhat relaxing.

During a morning Mass the week after I got back from Highlands, I heard Jesus direct me to feed his homeless people. I searched the internet for a place to volunteer. While I had volunteered in the past through my parish, none of the work involved interacting with the homeless. I made sandwiches and dropped them off at the church, boxed up food being sent out for various causes, and donated canned goods for food drives. But I felt that to do what Jesus was asking, I needed to have face-to-face interaction with the homeless.

I found a place called the Harvest Center and read their website to see exactly what they did. I was pleasantly surprised to discover that they not only served the homeless breakfast and lunch but also had transformation programs. There was a computer lab where homeless people could search for job opportunities and apartments. The center offered interview coaching, résumé help, and necessary life skills. They even had group homes where homeless individuals could live during periods of transformation. I loved their mission of getting people back on their feet rather than just feeding them and sending them back to the streets.

Based on my experience running a cleaning business, it was clear to me that many people try to meet the minimum work requirements so they can collect from the government. Let the rest of the world carry the weight, even when they are completely capable of contributing to society. The Harvest Center's approach was dynamic.

I started volunteering at the Harvest Center's Room at the Inn, where homeless men slept in the dining center during the cold winter months. It was rewarding, fun, and refreshing. The interaction was very natural, and they were genuinely thankful that I was there serving them. Once the winter ended, I started cooking and serving during lunchtime meals. Jesus was right; feeding his homeless brought great personal rewards. And contributing to an organization with wise long-term goals made good sense.

Shortly after I started working at the Harvest Center, I prayed, asking God whether I should give everything away as many saints had done in the past. Heaven was funneling through me so powerfully that seeking direction from God became my norm. God responded, "No, Amy, that's not my plan for you. But I don't think you need all the things you have. In fact, they seem to overwhelm you and stress you out. I want you to live simply enough to not be stressed. I want you to live abundantly in love, friendship, and family so you can move freely to share my message with the world."

A month later, around Christmastime, I went to a Christian music concert where a non-profit organization was looking for sponsors for needy children around the world. I already had eleven children in various countries who I sponsored through Compassion International but decided to sponsor another child. If God wanted me to feed his children, then I was going to do the best I could with the resources I had.

Then, a couple of days before Christmas while I was driving, I heard country music star, Jennifer Nettles, promoting a nonprofit organization called World Vision on the radio. One of World Vision's missions is to provide everyone in the world with clean water. The radio announcer was saying that while young boys were at school learning, the school-age girls would fetch water for the entire village. The young girls walked on average six miles each way carrying water to their village. This is what the girls were required to do instead of going to school! It infuriated me, and I immediately donated money to provide a water well to a village through World Vision. I have donated funds to build several more water wells in the past few years.

I wasn't speaking and proclaiming God's word yet, but I was definitely doing God's will. Communities not having clean drinking water in this day and age is irresponsible. There's no way God would find it acceptable for people to be without clean water. And making the girls fetch the water while the boys go to school?! Come on, people—that's barbaric.

The same fall, I attended the Eucharistic Congress uptown Charlotte in an attempt to participate fully in the Catholic Church where Jesus was holding me. Several bizarre things happened while I was there. The Eucharistic Congress took place during the time of the month when the Spirit was working through me so I was not "driving my own car." On arrival, I walked directly into the makeshift sacristy where the priests were getting dressed for the Mass and said hello to several of the priests from my parish. I was the only non-ordained individual in the room, but they were oddly welcoming. They didn't ask me to leave, instead acting as if I belonged there.

At lunchtime, I took the escalator up to grab a bite to eat at the food court in the convention center. On my way back down the escalator, I entered a room where thousands of people were listening to the Mass in Spanish. As I began to make my way through the masses of people, the priests surrounded me, and we proceeded through the crowds. There was no monstrance, but the priests surrounded me the same way they do during the processional to the altar with the body of Christ—as if I were the body of Christ. When we reached the end of the large auditorium, I walked through a door and back to the main hall where the English-speaking events were taking place. The priests surrounding me turned and walked, single file, to the altar at the front of the auditorium. Odd? Yes. Was I fazed? No.

I spotted a priest from my home parish and walked toward him, thinking that having a conversation with a familiar face might help ground me. As I approached him, he stepped behind a pillar in the auditorium but did not come out the other side. I quickly scoured the area with my eyes and could not find him anywhere. He seemed to vanish into thin air. At this point, I decided it was time to go home. I walked back over to the door that I had just exited where the Spanish Mass was in progress. I wanted to confirm that I had my feet on solid ground. I stepped back through the door to the Spanish-speaking auditorium, and there were only approximately 150 people in the room. I must have changed locations or dimensions somehow; there is no way several thousand people could have vacated that hall in a matter of two or three minutes. I was no longer sure if I had vanished into thin air and then reappeared or if the priest from my parish had vanished before my eyes!

I was perplexed, to say the least, but I was accustomed to my life feeling out of control. I went home and continued to live in each moment because I most definitely never knew what the next moment might bring.

The Spirit of the Lord is upon me because he has anointed me to bring glad tidings to the poor. He has sent me to proclaim liberty to captives and recovery of sight to the blind, to let the oppressed go free, and to proclaim a year acceptable to the Lord.
—Luke 4:18–19

Water Well

47 Saint Thérèse

Heaven's doors continued to open for me at least once a month. Wanting to figure out what my next step should be, I got busy reading about the saints in search of some commonalities. Unable to find a human being to compare my experiences with, I had to improvise. I decided to try to relate to people born in 1194, 1515, 1883, or 1887 in hopes of finding similarities to what I was experiencing. Not that doing so would get me out of my state of isolation, but like experiences would bolster my sanity. In addition, I would be able to speak about others with analogous mystical experiences.

I read about Saint Clare of Assisi, Saint Teresa of Ávila, Padre Pio, and Saint Thérèse of Lisieux and was relieved that I could relate to what they had experienced and felt. I must have either been born at the wrong time, or I've lived more than once—or maybe both. My research reminded me of a lucid dream I had a few months before in which a nun was petitioning Jesus on my behalf:

Dream

Last night, I woke at 3:00 a.m. and heard a sweet, high-pitched female voice say, "Stay calm, sweetheart; we are right here with you." Then a vision began. My body was physically in my bed on earth, but I was present in Spirit with the woman in my vision. She was a regal nun and appeared to be very important. Her high-pitched voice didn't match her tall, thick stature. She was standing facing the altar in the center aisle of an enormous cathedral. I was in an ancient wooden pew on the right side of the cathedral, kneeling. I wasn't on the kneeler, but on the actual pew like a child trying to elevate as high as I could to see what was going on. Something extraordinary was transpiring; I could feel it in my bones, and the smell of holy incense wafting through the air confirmed it.

A mammoth ivory pillar was blocking my view of the altar, but I knew Jesus was there because I was saturated with his essence. The nun was perfectly still with her hands folded in front of her. It appeared she was talking to Jesus in her mind as I often do, but she got to look directly at him. I was jealous but knew I was not worthy of standing where she was, so I stayed quiet and didn't move. I watched attentively like a child does when they want to be mature enough to participate. And those are not strong enough words to describe how desperate I was to be standing where the nun was.

I couldn't hear any of the conversation. I whispered to her, "Are you the one who I heard talking to me in my sleep a few minutes ago?" Without looking over at me or taking her eyes off Jesus, she said, "Yes, sweetheart, it was me." Then I whispered, "What is your name?" She didn't respond, so I just knelt on the wooden pew and watched her intense prayer and petition, which appeared to be on my behalf.

I drifted off to sleep for a few minutes before reawakening; I was no longer in the cathedral but in a hallway. I saw a door that was cracked open. I stepped forward into the room with my right foot up to my knee. I could feel the Holy Spirit sweep over my body, and I began to tingle. I heard a deeper male voice say, "Your foot is in the door." I drifted off again, and I saw a picture of an intricate engine. I had three clear visions. An engine picture flashed in my mind three times. The first time, most of the parts of the engine lit up red, indicating that they were working and warm; the second time, three parts lit up indicating they were repaired and ready to go; and then the last time, one part of the engine lit up blue, indicating it was still cold. It looked like the broken handle of a water spigot that only had two pieces of the dial left. I then heard the sweet nun say, "He is going up there to fix it." I lay in my bed, and my body got very hot; I began to sweat as if I was in a cooker oven. During this vision experience, I had several explosions of "light"—Heavenly light. In the beginning, I had several rays of light pour in through my left eye. Later, I received two large bursts of lights from above, one over my right eye and one between my eyes.

When I woke the next morning, I could feel Heaven starting to flow into my mind while my feet were on Earth, indicating my rise one day to new birth in God's Kingdom. Rising in the Kingdom would be spectacular because the isolation of being the only one to see, hear, and understand Heaven got old long ago. Befriending the spirits through studying the memories of deceased individuals was starting to bore me.

I had an epiphany one day when I was bored. My mind was slicing words into syllables when I realized that the English language was barbaric. As I thought about the word's cooker, washer, dryer, mower, blender, mixer, etc., my mind jumped to this: cook her, wash her, dry her, mow her, blend her, mix her, and so on. I had a serious laughing fit with tears rolling down my cheeks as I contemplated the stupidity of the English language, and it occurred to me that the language was created for the purpose of the purification of "woman." The "-er" words stand for "her," and are meant to describe the blending and purifying of the female. Either a man created this language or a woman who was trying to fix "man's" mistake. A woman would have created a language with the words cookim, washim, dryim, mowim, blendim, mixim, and so on. There are only two "-er" words that I can think of that I would keep if I were rewriting the language. The most important one being believer

—BELIEVE HER!

Otherwise, the English language is relatively primitive.

Anyway, I read several books written by saints and could easily relate to their experiences—especially their feelings of isolation and desperation to be with Jesus. I read the autobiography of Saint Thérèse of Lisieux and was shocked at how similar her story was to mine. She says in her book that weather patterns mirrored her emotions; the same occurs around me. When I initially noticed the weather followed my mood, I was in awe of the movements, but over time it became a norm:

The weather and my mood simply move together.

Saint Thérèse of Lisieux also had a desperate need to try to catch the blood of Jesus Christ at the base of the cross, as did I for many years. I am not aware of anyone else who has had the same experience, and it started occurring long before I ever read Saint Thérèse's autobiography and discovered that she had similar occurrences. I wasn't successful at catching Jesus's blood on both sides of the cross until Charles helped me during a vision I had at Mass one day by kneeling at the other side of the cross, holding his own chalice to complete the insurmountable task. A task I had painfully visualized so many times.

Saint Thérèse also connected the events of her life to Biblical Scripture, as do I. She was clearly a more devout Christian than I am, and let's face it, she probably had lips of honey. I can't say the same about the words that come out of my mouth, but I am likely more fun to hang out with. Saint Thérèse prayed for death so she could be with Jesus and got her wish at a very young age. If I am candid, I have prayed for death many times over the past seven years, but God has not granted me that wish. My suffering for the cross must not be completed. Saint Thérèse of Lisieux lost her buckle at Assisi, and I lost mine in college. And, most interestingly to me, Jesus took the cup of suffering back from Saint Thérèse and didn't let her finish it, just as he has done with me. Not that he won't give it back to me; who knows?

Not long after reading Saint Thérèse's story, I had a conversation with Jesus in the upper room of my mind:

I went to the upper room of my mind and sat with Jesus. He seemed happy to see me. I sat next to him, and he laid his hands firmly on mine, interlacing our fingers. He leaned over, kissed my cheek, then said to me, "You will endure." I took a deep breath and said, "I know. I would do anything for you, but I am much ornerier than Saint Thérèse."

Salvation

Jesus didn't laugh or smile, so I became serious. He asked me to say my mantra, so I did: "I am the beloved servant of Jesus Christ, his sister, his bride, Lady Zion, and the one predicted by the prophet Isaiah. Begone evil spirits or I will summon my husband." Afterward, I asked Jesus about Saint Thérèse; her story made complete sense to me, and I could see multiple parallels between our lives. I said to Jesus, "Saint Thérèse lost her buckle, was handed a cup of suffering, and then you took the cup away from her. Her relationship with you developed on a very similar path to mine. So how is my journey different from hers?"

Still serious, Jesus looked at me and said, "You were still too soft; you had not gone far enough underground to endure." Then he asked, "What did you say in your mantra that is different from Saint Thérèse's story?" I replied, "That I am the fulfillment of the prophet Isaiah?" Jesus looked at me and said, "Yes, that's right, my love. Jesus had to take the cup back because it wasn't time."

Puzzled, I looked at Jesus and said, "You are Jesus."

He replied, "I am, and you are."

See, upon the mountains there advances the bearer of good news, announcing peace! Celebrate your feasts, O Judah, fulfill your vows! For nevermore shall you be invaded by the scoundrel; he is completely destroyed. The Lord will restore the vine of Jacob, the pride of Israel, though ravagers have ravaged them and ruined the tendrils.
—Nahum 2:1-3

48 Birthing Pains

The heavens are overrated

Is heaven overrated?
My dreams left unanswered.

Revelation flowing through me makes me question if I matter. Made an empty vessel to fix those heaven decided to rescatter.

Stars rise above and settle in the east.

Me left broken and shattered, scrambling for each piece. A spirit from above, operating through me from beyond, thanks me for my sacrifice; The sacrifice made to free her tethered daughters.

The ones she believes deserve to be released.

Me, a flow-through
pawn,
left isolated and
caged like a beast.

My purpose still undefined. No sight of being unbound. The call I answered has destroyed what I once found—The piece of Heaven I grasped now lost to a voice holding me down.

Set
apart in a
bubble exiled,
I sit and watch
the world go
around.

My relationships all synthetic, the ones that made me thrive.

Tugged in motion from above,

while held underground.

Erratic movements in multiple directions, scramble my thoughts.
Poked and prodded like a voodoo doll,

encompassing the earth.

The Whole World

Made to spin in circles,

in hopes of delivering power from Heaven down to earth.

With my four years in heaven's virtual prison coming to an end, I knew I was heading into the "office" or "work" phase of my seven-year exile. Physical sensations of pain in my hands, feet, and side became less frequent. Most of the time, I could feel a shackle on my left ankle, but it was intermittent.

What escalated was the reconstruction of my body. I could feel God repairing my spinal cord where the electric shock had radiated up my back almost twenty years before. Little jolts of electricity started shooting through my extremities. Sensation was coming back to my fingers, toes, and the bottoms of my feet. The pain and tightness in my neck, where my thyroid gland is, was starting to heal. I could physically feel my body rhythmically rebuilding from the inside out.

The other thing that was flourishing was the clarity, detail, and frequency of my dreams, visions, and understanding.

Dream

> I had a dream one morning in which I was sitting on a tall concrete block wall with Saint Peter and Saint Paul. We were high up in the sky, talking and trying to figure out how to get down. Saint Peter started to scale down the side of the wall when it began to rain heavily. Saint Paul and I were still talking and trying to figure out how to get to Saint Peter. As we began to scale the wall, it folded in half, and we were all safely on the ground together. Heaven on Earth happens;   We all converge—I'm positive.

When I woke from the dream, a dream I had several months prior popped into my mind. I was talking with some angels in heaven and refusing to give up Buck or leave Charles behind; I simply would not thread the eye of the needle and enter God's Kingdom without everybody I loved. The angels were frustrated with how stubborn I was being, but I refused to budge.

My mind roamed back to Buck again. During the first year of my prison sentence when the Lord was overshadowing me, I got up in the middle of the night and decided to watch some old home DVDs. The first DVD I put on was a video Charles took of the house we had built in Pennsylvania prior to the installation of sheetrock. The video was of the inside of all the walls with the electrical wires and pipes exposed. As I was watching the beginning of that video, I heard Buck say, "I was hoping we would have a house together one day." At the time, I freaked out, not knowing where Buck's voice was coming from, and I quickly turned the video off. Then I heard Buck say, "I guess that's never going to happen." A wave of sadness came over me, realizing that it hadn't happened for us and that Buck said it never would.

How is it that I hear Buck's voice in my head?

I don't think I realized at the time that his voice was in my head, but it must have been because I had already turned the DVD off when I heard him talking to me. My inability to keep thoughts of Buck out of my mind is exhausting;

why am I unable to break this annoying chain?

I decided to open my Bible and look for an answer from God as to what I should do to break the chain. Using "Bible roulette," the pages fell open, and my eyes fell here:

Thorns

*Therefore, I will hedge in her way with thorns
    and erect a wall against her,
    so that she cannot find her paths.*

*If she runs after her lovers, she will not overtake them;
    if she looks for them she shall not find them.
Then she will say,
    "I will go back to my first husband,
    for it was better with me then than now."
So I will allure her;
    I will lead her into the desert
    and speak to her heart.*

*From there I will give her the vineyards she had,
and the valley of Achor as a door of hope.*

*She shall respond there as in the days of her youth,
when she came up from the land of Egypt.
On that day, says the Lord,
    She shall call me "My husband,"
    and never again "My baal."*

*Then will I remove from her mouth the
    names of the Baals,*

Grapevine

so that they shall no longer be invoked.
I will make a covenant for them on that day,
with the beasts of the field,
With the birds of the air,
and with the things that crawl on the ground.

Scorpion

Bow and sword and war
I will destroy from the land,
and I will let them take their rest in security.
I will espouse you to me forever:
I will espouse you in right and in justice,
I will espouse you in fidelity,
and you shall know the Lord .

Sword

On that day I will respond—says the Lord —

I will respond to the heavens,
and they will respond to the earth;
The earth will respond to the grain, and wine, and oil,
and these will respond to Jezreel.
I will sow him for myself in the land,
and I will have pity on Lo-ruhama ...
I will say to Lo-ammi, "You are my people,"
and he shall say, "My God!"
—Hosea 2:8-25

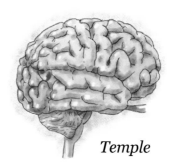

Temple

Go back to my first?
Would I really go back to Buck?
Is that what God is telling me?

While there were so many things about being with Buck that I loved, it seemed impossible.

We were both married to other people on earth.

I researched this Scripture and discovered that the Valley of Achor is a place where trouble opens the door to a new hope. Could I or should I even hope to be with Buck? I was confident that he had powerful Spiritual gifts from Heaven based on several facts. First, our eternal Divine connection was confirmed for me by the letter I found from our childhood, which contained words that transcended time. Also, the prophetic words Buck spoke to me during our reunion and his continued presence in my lucid dreams and encounters in Heaven.

Why were mystical things not occurring with my legal, earthly husband? Charles must not have the gifts required to enter the Promised Land in his head yet. This thought panicked me until I reread the Scripture, *"I will sow him for myself in the land."* (Hosea 2:25) I felt confident that God was going to fix the Promised Land in Charles's brain so that he, too, could enter God's Kingdom.

Determined not to leave anyone I loved behind, I remained adamant that I would not pass through the eye of the needle unless they came with me. Leaving a single soul behind was unacceptable.

Achor

49 I Loved You through My Broken Heart

Your Spirit towered over me, majestic and true.
It drew me in perfectly to a place I never knew.
Love flowed freely from a kindness rarely seen.
Holding me safely in a sacred place to lean.

The perfect place to raise a family.
We added three happy little boys.
Love, loyalty, and safety surrounded me each day,
In a way I never imagined, or am able to convey.

As we uprooted and replanted, our joy continued to flourish.
You a sturdy anchor and me here to nourish.
The three gifts we were given we didn't understand,
The power we had under the master's spectacular plan.

When the boys became young men, and your work kept us apart,
A pain from my past, lingering in my heart,
Gnawed at me daily, and loneliness grew fast.
My mind started to wander in search of a new start.

I sent a prayer up above to save our precious love.
The spinning of my mind sent me soaring like a dove,
And when the heavens answered, my work got very hard.
Where it quickly became apparent, you were my special guard.

I scoured the universe, collecting the pieces of my heart,
Only to discover the one I gave you was broken from the start.
Unconscious of the tear, I dove in completely unaware,

My brokenness was something we would jointly share.

With purity, strength, and loyalty our union gave birth,
to a Divine union I'm confident will bring Heaven down to Earth,
My memories of love and happiness, nothing can abate.
Even though at the finish, we felt agony and heartache.

My love was sincere from my state of repose,
A life I would never trade, in spite of its end.
A higher call we had right from the start.
Our story—God's perfect art.

You a pure treasure, a tower that stands tall.
Me too green to reach it, having searched along my fall.
When my father said we must be rescattered,
with great sadness ... I left your side.

Your sanctuary determined no longer my resting place.
I aspire to be more like you as I work hard without haste.
Our union will be considered,
most assuredly not a waste.

Joy, love, and happiness are the memories I carry forward,
A life beautifully lived, I treasure each day.
As we step in new directions, I want the very best,
For both of us finally, as we deserve rest.

My heart torn in pieces, cracked from my past.
I'm off to pick them up, find Heaven, and fill the holes at last.
I loved you through my broken heart, the depths of which are vast.
My biggest regret in life is that I broke your precious heart.

Husbands, love your wives, just as Christ loved the church and gave himself up for her, in order to make her holy by cleansing her with the washing of water by the word, so as to present the church to himself in splendor, without a spot or wrinkle or anything of the kind—yes, so that she may be holy and without blemish.
—Ephesians 5:25-27

Wedding

50 Blameless

Morning Mass continued to be a daily desire; I wanted to meet Jesus, and I could hear and feel him powerfully at Mass. For whatever reason, priests started to behave oddly during Mass; one day, all the priests laid down on the altar with a small crucifix in their hands. The next Sunday, the priest sat down before the banquet table was cleared. Priests' behavior was intermittently odd. I decided it was part of the process of trying to confuse me to grow the temple in my brain so I could be fixed. They needed me to do my job. Or maybe they were trying to confuse everybody who was entering God's Kingdom? I wasn't sure, but the universe seemed to need the information in my head, the archives—an ark filled with a mother lode of information.

Why else would everybody be working so hard to fix me?

I would hear Jesus in my head during the priest's random actions telling me what to do during Mass, and I would listen to Him. I always chalked up how I reacted to the erratic behavior to "I'm not driving my own car today—Jesus has the wheel." But after the Mass was over, I would worry whether I had done something wrong. Did I say the words to a prayer wrong? Or go up for communion when I shouldn't have? Did I stand up when I should have knelt? Not that I cared what people in the pews thought, but I didn't want to mess anything up for Jesus.

After one of those weird mornings at Mass, I went straight to see Jesus in the upper room of my mind. He reached for my hand and walked me over to the couch, where we sat down. I said, "I'm worried that I keep messing up; what is wrong with me?" Jesus looked right at me, gently lifted my chin so my eyes met His, and said, "You didn't mess anything up, my love. Remember, you turned yourself over to me entirely. Your eyes are fixed on me, and that is precisely what I planned. You, my delight, are perfect and completely blameless."

How could I be blameless with all the pain I had recently inflicted on the people I love? And what about the mistakes I have made in my life? This made no sense. I stood up and started crying, just thinking that I would never want to hurt Charles, but still, I kept picking Buck every time I circled trying to break this final chain. Jesus looked at me and said,

Cage With No Door

"What about what you want?"

I asked God many years ago to make me love Charles more than Buck, but that was not happening. At least not yet. I suppose I never got my heart back from Buck. What do I want? I started to contemplate this question daily but was unable to find a resolution that allowed me to get what I wanted without hurting anyone. I guess some things can't be figured out.

I am trapped in conflicts between heaven and earth that can't be resolved, and there is no escape. The church and the government say I am married to Charles, while God and the Bible say I am married to Buck. It doesn't matter because Buck says he's married to someone else, and Charles believes he's married to me. Jesus says I'm a priestess and must stay in the Catholic Church, and the Catholic Church, of course, refuses to allow a woman to enter the seminary and become a priest. Quite the obstruction to standing behind the banquet table or preaching a sermon in the Catholic Church on earth, don't you think?

I'm in a cage with no door.

I want to get to Heaven and fast.

This world is emptiness.

I can't realize my dreams or the dreams of Jesus Christ.

170

I would spend the next several months thinking about what I wanted. Mothers in general, and me for sure, spend most of our time meeting others' needs instead of making our own a priority. I hadn't thought for years about what I wanted. Not until that fatal question the salesman asked me when I decided to go back to work in corporate America (and look where that got me). What did I want out of life and a career? What were my dreams and aspirations? The salesman's question ignited a flame that sent me into this tailspin where I still remain—locked away toiling while others hijack my mind gathering information.

And it is my prayer that your love may abound more and more, with knowledge and all discernment, so that you may approve what is excellent, and may be pure and blameless for the day of Christ, filled with the fruits of righteousness which come through Jesus Christ, to the glory and praise of God.
—Philippians 1:9–11

51 What Do I Want?

And I will bring the third part through the fire, refine them as silver is refined, and test them as gold is tested. They will call on My name, And I will answer them; I will say, "They are My people," And they will say, "The Lord is my God."
—Zechariah 13:9

What Do I Want?

To do the job my **Father** in Heaven sent me to do—I hate to not follow through.
To write a book that expands God's Kingdom—one people will read.
That shouts out Heaven's message—a message many desperately need.

For my **son**s to be proud of me—so they have a clue what a strong woman can do.
For all to understand—that life is not always what you plan.
So, faith in the Kingdom is ultimately what you have.

To not hurt anyone in the process—that didn't happen.
To make sure they know—I tried hard not to let go.
Because at the end of the day—it would be nice if everybody could stay.

For the world to be a better place—where children are safe.
For moms and dads to come home at night—and have a family life.
That's the way God planned it—loved ones stay in one place.

To stay on the horse—when I decide to canter.
To round the barrel in step—the way that God meant.
Because if that happened—all promises would be kept.

For my sister to get well—she has been through enough hell.
For her lungs to fill with air—and her brain to repair.

So she can enjoy her growing family—now that would be fair.

To fly on aerial hammocks—just like Pink.
To accept what's on my mind—and say what I think.
Then to speak my truth—even if it stinks.

For kids to not be bullied—life is hard enough.
For those who clearly see it—to call it out in stride.
Then maybe these frequent killings—would cease to exist.

To travel around the world—understanding what others face.
To work to make life better—for those missing Heaven's taste.
Because at the end of the day—we are all one human race.

For color not to matter—skin is simply not that deep.
For if you look through it—the **Spirit** will clearly speak.
Because every life should matter—that's why Jesus was made weak.

For all the scales to fall from my eyes—my transformation complete.
For the pain in my side to alleviate—and the throbbing in my feet.
So, I reach the full stature of Christ—and this process never repeat.

To stop spinning in circles—with always the same result.
To accept that I always return—to the very place I start.
Because I see things so clearly—apparently, I'm quite smart.

For Buck to love me—the way he promised.
For my dreams to come true—and maybe his too.
Because some things were meant to be—decided before the start.

To get my words down on paper—and have them all make sense.
To hold the hardbound cover—I know it was Heaven sent.

Because after all this spinning—I would like a happy event.

For everyone to have food—and clean drinking water.
For passion to determine purpose—in lieu of building wealth.
Then humans would feel more joy—and need less medicinal help.

To stand before a crowd—and speak out loud.
To be confident in what I am saying—and not covered in a cloud.
Because that's the job I was assigned—when my stars were aligned.

For the world around me to see—who I was meant to be.
For people to finally approach me—and ask me what I see.
Then I will escape this bubble—and reenter society.

To break right through the ceiling—shattering all the glass.
To ring the church bells so loudly—I annihilate everything in hell.
Then Jesus' sacrifice—would result in a beautiful place to dwell.

Though one may be overpowered, two can defend themselves. A cord of three strands is not quickly broken.
—Ecclesiastes 4:12

Braid of Three

52 Frequent Conversations

After Buck texted me about my car while I was in Maine, the frequency of our communication increased. It was the fall of 2018, and we started to talk on the phone, text, or email maybe once a week. And when the Spirit was blowing through me, I would "vomit" my emotions all over him. Communication between us progressed slowly at first. I started by sharing a few of my poems and meditations with him. The meditations and poems were Spiritual or religious. For example, I shared this poem and explained to Buck that it was about my Spiritual journey with Jesus:

My Delight

Halfway between Heaven and earth is where I'm in my perfect light
Just you and me soaring one level out of sight;
Floating just above the surface is where I want to be.
You and me passing, where no one else can see;
You, my perfect lover, and I, soon your delight.
We soar above the earth, transcending time and space;
riding just above the surface—the perfect hiding place.
For you, my perfect lover, and me your ever delight.
It's a place no one can touch us, where you woo me with new sight.
Such joy you've planned out for us when we reach our glorious height.

Buck responded via email by saying that if the poem were put in another context, it could be about a human man rather than Jesus. **How should I take this?** I wasn't sure but thought he might be speaking of himself.

After a few phone conversations, I sent Buck the picture of the two of us in high school and shared my theories—that the books behind my head contained the information that Heaven dumped into my mind a few years ago when I was in the hospital; that Buck's shirt was white, indicating that he was purified; and that my shirt was black, meaning that I was still covered in sin. I let Buck know that I was having trouble getting rid of him as I kept spinning through the wash-and-spin cycle in the refiner's fire. He responded via email that he was sorry to keep disturbing my spin cycles.

Could Buck be doing this to me on purpose? I have heard Buck's voice in my head. **Is he holding onto me?** I think I liked the idea of Buck holding onto me when clearly, I shouldn't.

A few weeks passed, and in response to one of our phone conversations, I emailed him a picture of the letter he sent me during college, explaining to him the connections I had made between his college love letter and what was happening to me now in the Spiritual dimension during purification.

"But as it is written, they shall see who have never been told of him, and they shall see who have never heard of him." This is the reason why I have so often been hindered from coming to you. But now, since I no longer have any room for work in these regions, and since I have longed for many years to come to you, I hope to see you.
—Romans 15:21–22

Norman Rockwell

53 Acceptable Behavior?

Up to this point, communication between Buck and me was within the lines of acceptable behavior for a man and woman married to other people. Our interaction was more of an investigation of what was going on with me spiritually—one old friend helping another.

Could Buck validate the connections I was making?

Buck was giving me a hand.

All the things I considered potentially inappropriate on Buck's part could have been in my mind. Maybe he meant them innocently, or perhaps I was reading something into his words that weren't there.

A few days later, Buck's response to the college love letter I emailed him crossed the line that I had been skirting around. He said, "After reading the letter I wrote, you should have written me off as crazy long ago. Madly in love or just gone mad? Maybe the chains you have to break run from me to you and not the reverse."

My heart started to race; inside I felt elated, but my mind was freaking out. Dammit, I did not want to feel like this. I was not surprised about how I felt; deep down, I knew I had been hiding from my longing for Buck for a lifetime. But I was shocked at how Buck felt. That he was holding onto me—chains running from him to me! And yes, I most definitely liked it.

I decided to try to lighten the interaction and replied by mentioning some additional connections I made from our childhood that related to my current life events. I told him:

• First, that he always used to tell me that I was the sweetest person he ever met, and that is what Jesus tells me during our conversations in the upper room of my mind.

• Second, that he used to say when we were kids that I was the kind of person who grew more beautiful with age. And if Jesus is resurrecting me, then I will undoubtedly be more appealing once the rotting odor of sin is stripped from me.

177

- Finally, that he had written two rules on my whiteboard in college: Rule 1: Buck is always right. Rule 2: If Buck is wrong, then refer to Rule 1.

I added that at this point, we would need to change the names in the rules from "Buck" to "Amy" since I was the one interacting with Heaven and not him—at least as far as I was aware.

Lady Liberty

Not long after, Buck emailed me a picture my mom had given him when we were in college. I was pleasantly surprised that he had saved it—not something a guy would typically do. The coin at the end of the chain is a 1924 twenty-dollar piece with an eagle on one side, and on the other side, Lady Liberty holding the tree of life while standing on a rock. I had misplaced that necklace a few years back and then randomly found it a couple of days after Buck sent me the picture … Odd.

Lady Liberty, a rock, an eagle, and the tree of life
are linked directly to my interactions with Heaven over the past several years.

Law or Faith

O stupid Galatians! Who has bewitched you, before whose eyes Jesus Christ was publicly portrayed as crucified? I want to learn only this from you: did you receive the Spirit from works of the law, or from faith in what you heard? Are you so stupid? After beginning with the Spirit, are you now ending with the flesh? Did you experience so many things in vain?—if indeed it was in vain. Does, then, the one who supplies the Spirit to you and works mighty deeds among you do so from works of the law or from faith in what you heard? Thus Abraham "believed God, and it was credited to him as righteousness."
—Galatians 3:1–6

54 Break the Chain

I guess that Buck revealing in his email that he had not let go of me when he commented that the chains ran from him to me—and revealing that he had held onto our childhood memories—was enough to tip the scales for me. Enough for me to take a leap of faith and tell him how I felt about him, still, after all these years. I asked him to call me, and I sat in my car in a parking lot one day while we talked. I started by asking him what he meant by the chains running from him to me.

Buck was evasive by just repeating the words that he had written in his email.

How annoying.

He told me during our conversation that he thought I had my mother's eyes. My mom knew what was going to happen before it happened most of the time, just like I do. I knew exactly what Buck was telling me: my eyes are not physically like hers, but I have her gift to "see" Spiritually. I think my mom was far more beautiful.

Then Buck continued the conversation by bringing up a weird kid from college. He pointed out that he would never have left me alone with the boy.

Was Buck trying to tell me that he is my "Jesus"?

Jesus continually said to me that he would not leave me alone but would stay with me while I am tested in the fire. I brushed that thought away quickly, deciding that the understanding and revelation that I have received from Jesus are far beyond Buck's capability.

Jacqueline Jean

Besides, the dreams, words, and perfection of the romance that I have with Jesus are outside of Buck's wheelhouse, at least the Buck I remember from my youth. Buck is an engineer with a logical mind—

a mind that tossed me away years ago.

However, the conversations Buck and I were having did feel protective and out of character for someone supposedly married to and in love with another woman. My head was now spinning in circles in two different directions at the same time.

I decided to leap again, and I told Buck that I didn't want to break the chain and would prefer that he not break it either. I said I had loved him from eternity somehow and could hear him in my head sometimes and often saw him in my dreams. I confessed that I never recovered from his leaving me behind and wished he had come to get me when he saw in the newspaper that I was getting married.

Buck responded by saying he regretted that he had not come to get me —he wished he had.

The desperation in his voice as he strained to get those words out confirmed his love for me.

I continued the conversation by telling Buck that it wasn't that I didn't love my husband because Charles is a great man. But there was a connection beyond my understanding that I had with Buck that I could never recover from or shake. I told Buck that I had three problems, and he was deeply entwined in all of them:

Number one, I want to do what God sent me to do.
Number two, I don't want to hurt anyone.
And number three, it is impossible for me not to love him.

At that, Buck got uncomfortable and said he had to go. I quickly mentioned to him that through my dreams and revelation, I was confident that the Holy bloodline was on Earth now. He repeated back to me quizzically, "the Holy bloodline?" I responded, "Yes," slightly annoyed that nobody ever seems to want to believe me. Buck quickly said goodbye and hung up.

Great, I thought to myself. I finally unload this weight, and Buck retreats. Maybe this will be the rejection that releases me from the chain that is binding me to my childhood sweetheart and making me feel utterly ridiculous. This must be the reason women should not have sex before marriage. The bond that is created with a woman's "first" is too strong to break.

It is ruining my life and making me crazy—literally.

I spent the entire night thinking about Buck's words, my words, and what was wrong with me.

Why am I so stupid when it comes to Buck?

Especially when I have a husband who has been faithful to me for so many years?

The New Zion

Raise a glad cry, you barren one who did not bear, break forth in jubilant song, you who were not in labor, for more numerous are the children of the deserted wife than the children of her who has a husband, says the Lord. Enlarge the space for your tent, spread out your tent clothes unsparingly; lengthen your ropes and make firm your stakes. For you shall spread abroad to the right and to the left; your descendants shall dispossess the nations and shall people the desolate cities. Fear not, you shall not be put to shame; you need not blush, for you shall not be disgraced. The shame of your youth you shall forget, the reproach of your widowhood no longer remembered. For he who has become your husband is your Maker; his name is the Lord of hosts; Your redeemer is the Holy One of Israel, called God of all the earth. The Lord calls you back, like a wife forsaken and grieved in spirit, a wife married in youth and then cast off, says your God. For a brief moment I abandoned you, but with great tenderness I will take you back. In an outburst of wrath, for a moment I hid my face from you, says the Lord your redeemer. This is for me like the days of Noah, when I swore that the waters of Noah should never again deluge the earth; so, I have sworn not to be angry with you, or to rebuke you. Though the mountains leave their place and the hills be shaken, my love shall never leave you nor my covenant of peace be shaken, say the Lord, who has mercy on you. O afflicted one, storm-battered and unconsoled, I lay your pavements in carne-

lians, and your foundations in sapphires; I will make your battlements of rubies, your gates of carbuncles, and all your walls of precious stones. All your sons shall be taught by the Lord, and great shall be the peace of your children. In justice shall you be established, far from the fear of oppression, where destruction cannot come near you. Lo, I have created the craftsman who blows on the burning coals and forges weapons as his work; It is I also who have created the destroyer to work havoc. No weapon fashioned against you shall prevail; every tongue you shall prove false that launches an accusation against you. This is the lot of the servants of the Lord, their vindication from me, says the Lord.
—Isaiah 54:1-17

Music

55 Nothing Left

I gave a man my heart and soul; others took my dignity and wealth.
Left under a bushel, waiting for the universe to snuff me out.
What do people want from me?
—There's nothing left.

Tossed aside by the love of my life, was I his lover or his wife?
Emotionally abused and abhorred, left never to be adored.
A blonde in fancy pants, a redhead with bigger boobs.
Don't I have what's required
—to ever be your muse?

Blonde Barbie

A stay-at-home mom,
no fancy career or patents in my name.
No miraculous success stories
—to grace your ears.

How was the furniture divided?
How dare you even ask!
If you knew the words that left his lips
—that question never would have been asked.

The woman from heaven who thanked me,
her daughters now protected,
She didn't ask my opinion,
—I guess it doesn't count.

Redhead Barbie

Thankfully God decided
to send his only son,
and Jesus died to save me
—and chose me as his own.

If I can reach Jesus,
the lights of Heaven will shine,
and all will finally see
the woman and the beauty that God intended me to be.

The Lord GOD, who gathers the outcasts of Israel, declares, "Yet others I will gather to them, to those already gathered."
—Isaiah 56:8

Table and Chair

56 The Wedding Garment

He who has an ear, let him hear what the Spirit says to the churches. To him who over-comes, I will grant to eat of the tree of life which is in the Paradise of God.
—Revelation 2:7

Dream

Last night, when I got to Heaven, Jesus and I sat on an enormous concrete ledge. The wall rose all the way to Heaven, and we had one leg draped over each side of the wall. On one side of the wall, we looked down at the earth, and on the other, we looked over at Heaven.

It was a beautiful night; the stars spanned the dark sky. Jesus spoke the sweet-est words to me. I could feel his love penetrating right through me, and I could tell that he was pleased with me by his soft smile and gentle touch. I asked Je-sus why He was so pleased tonight, and, in response, he asked a question of his own: "What do you think you are doing that is pleasing to me?" I thought for a minute and said, "I am loving you and spending time with you." Jesus smiled, saying, "Yes, that makes me very happy. Tell me more, because there are at least a hundred things right now that are pleasing to me about you." I pondered only a few minutes and then started to rattle off as many things as I could think of: I am obedient to you, I go to Mass every day, I have my eyes fixed on you, Scripture is rolling off my lips daily, I am feeding the hungry, I am providing water for the poor, I am not worrying about money because it all belongs to you anyway, I am showing kindness to my neighbor, I am loving my family ... I went on for a while until he grabbed both of my hands, leaned in, and kissed me. It was gentle, and my entire body was electrified.

Jesus pulled me forward and motioned for me to turn around so that I was leaning my body back against his. He wrapped his arms around me. We sat for a few minutes looking at the magnificence of what he had created. I sat in awe as I relaxed my body right into his. Jesus asked me what I saw when I looked down at the earth that made me sad. I was spending most of my time looking toward Heaven because I was happier there. I sat and thought for a minute before I started to speak. "There are priests who represent you who are violating children and going unpunished; there are men physically and emotionally abusing women and getting away with it; there are children who are hungry and thirsty and nobody is providing nourishment; there are children who are being bullied and isolated that turn to violence, killing your people; there are mentally ill people who are left wandering the streets and nobody helps them; there are people who are lazy and won't lift a finger to do anything for themselves but expect a free ride; there are single mothers who are raising their children on their own while deadbeat dads run around with younger women and fail to provide support for their families; there are people walking around with their heads in their phones and on social media who don't interact with one another and develop meaningful relationships; there are old people who are lonely and left without purpose; there are people who don't bother to love, praise, and honor you or spend time with you, and they are missing out on the best part of life." I stopped at that, and with tears rolling down my cheeks, I twisted around and looked at Jesus and said, "That is why I like to look at Heaven instead. I am happier with you." I turned back to lean my head against his chest, and he wrapped his arms around me tightly and said, "Close your eyes, sweetheart, and get some sleep now."

When I woke up, we stood up, each with one leg on either side of the concrete wall;
the ground was below both of my feet:
Heaven on Earth—time was standing still.
The leaves danced in the air, defying gravity, and nobody seemed surprised.

Dancing Leaves

At the time of my "vomit" conversation with Buck, I was reading a book by Cynthia Bourgeault called The Meaning of Mary Magdalene. She talks about how male and female become one by connecting their minds. This connection is the "wedding garment" that is referred to in Scripture, according to the book. While reading the description, I began to think about the reconstruction of the temple in my brain—the "tree of life." I contemplated whether Buck had reached the summit of his tree of life, and that is how I hear his voice in my head. Could this be? Jesus did tell me years ago in a dream that he was married to Mary Magdalene and that she was doing the work God sent her to do, but unfortunately, the world had discounted her value. Maybe Jesus and Mary Magdalene were connected through their minds also—

two towers whose lobbies were connected!

Two Towers' Lobbies Connected

The gospel of Saint Thomas indicates that Jesus planned to make Mary Magdalene into a living spirit one day. If the world wouldn't accept Mary Magdalene, Jesus said he would right the wrongs and make two become one. The male becomes female, and the female becomes male, by joining themselves through their minds—a transformation enabling them to hear one another's thoughts. Beloveds are able to do so by reading or hearing your beloved's thoughts by using your entire brain once you reach the summit of the tree of life and enter God's Kingdom.

A unitive or transformed being;

Two become one and have a singular mind.

I find this possibility mind-boggling. A few years ago, I was just an ordinary woman, and now maybe I am something more.

A living spirit?

Mary Magdalene?

A unitive, transformed being ... connected to Buck?

I'm not entirely sure who or what I am at this point, but I am exhausted, tired of exile, and sick of this virtual cage where no definitive answers exist or dreams can be realized.

The day after my "vomit" conversation with Buck, I received an email from him. He apologized for the abrupt ending to our conversation, saying he needed to contemplate what I had said. Classic—just run and hide. Then Buck went on in the email in bullet-point format to tell me that over the years he has had the feeling that I needed him or was in trouble. I thought, well then why the hell didn't you find me?

Then in the next sentence, Buck said he tried a few times to find me, but my last name is common so he couldn't. He continued by sharing that he had obsessed at times over me in the past twenty-eight years and was not sure if it was boyhood, worldly love, or higher love. Finally, he proclaimed that he would or could never love anyone as much as he loved me, and quite frankly hadn't. That was enough.

Joy washed over me; I was bathed in the security of eternal love. I released the air from my lungs that I had been holding in from the moment I opened the email. I felt sure that Buck knew what was going on with me, and maybe he had experienced his own trip through hell, dance with the devil, and transformation.

We spoke again a few days later, and he reminded me of something we did together the very last time we saw each other twenty-eight years ago at his sister's apartment. He indicated that I had given him a gift when we got in his sister's jet tub and chatted that night before parting ways. It quickly popped into my head that I had sanctified him—cleansed Buck of all wrongdoing toward me so we could be together later. How I knew to do that is beyond me. But I was saving Buck for later—or maybe Heaven was saving him for me.

Let this mind be in you, that was also in Christ Jesus.
—Philippians 2:5

57 Pick Our Birthdates

The Lord spoke to Moses, saying: Speak to the people of Israel, saying: If a woman conceives and bears a male child, she shall be ceremonially unclean seven days; as at the time of her menstruation, she shall be unclean. On the eighth day the flesh of his foreskin shall be circumcised. Her time of blood purification shall be thirty-three days; she shall not touch any holy thing, or come into the sanctuary, until the days of her purification are completed. If she bears a female child, she shall be unclean two weeks, as in her menstruation; her time of blood purification shall be sixty-six days.
—Leviticus 12:1-5

Did we pick our birthdates?

I was born on 11/11/66 and was confident that being born on Veterans Day, along with having all those ones in my birthdate, was lucky. I am not so sure anymore. I can make almost all the numbers of the birthdates of significant people in my life mean something in Scripture and in my life. In fact, I seem to be able to make everything add up and circle back to me these days. It feels more like a curse than a blessing.

In 1999, when the shock that went up my spine closing off access to parts of my mind, I was 33 years old. Jesus was 33 when he was crucified, and 33 happens to be the number of days it takes for a woman to be purified after giving birth to a son. I was born in 1966, and 66 is the number of days it takes for a woman to be cleansed after giving birth to a daughter, primarily because the mother must redeem herself and her daughter because "woman" has not been cleansed. A boy is cleansed because Jesus died and purified the male; Jesus died so all could rise one day, Jesus purifying mankind. Therefore, when a daughter is born, the mother must endure 33 days for herself and an additional 33 days for her daughter—woman not cleansed.

If I am who Jesus tells me I am—the fulfillment of the prophet Isaiah, the Mother of all mothers, "Woman"—then all women will be purified if I do my job. It's entirely possible that the 11/11 in my birthdate suggests a whole cleansed man and a whole cleansed woman for the second time in history. The first time both were cleansed was with Jesus, Mary, and Joseph, and now with

Amy, Buck, and Charles (ABC's– letters matter too). The numbers matter and everybody that was here when Jesus, Mary, and Joseph were, are here again. I have continually said that the numbers matter, but nobody will listen to me—"just" a Woman. Assuming I am right, let's hope humanity won't screw this up again and decide to play games with life, because I won't do this job again … *ever*.

Now, because I think too much, I have contemplated that if things fall in order, I will die at the age of 66 because Jesus died at the age of 33. Unless I get back the years that the locusts took from me, which is what the prophet Isaiah predicted. Then I regain 21 years of life (from 1999 to 2020, which is perfect vision) or 33 years, which is the number of years from 1987—when I was stung by a bee after Buck dumped me to date the blonde—until 2020. Either way, if I get the years back that the locusts took, then I will be damn old when I die. Who knows? I've decided to live in the moment, so I won't dwell on getting back lost time, but I do hope to see my grandchildren. My mom and dad didn't get to meet my sons. I plan to spoil my grandchildren rotten.

My sister was born on Labor Day, which adds up. Her head started to scab over with MS a year after our mom died. What was happening? I would guess her temple was being laid bare by prayers flowing through her mind to the heavens. Then, after years of suffering, she contracted a disease that causes her lungs to scab over, and now she labors to breathe—she is on oxygen. Yep, that sure sounds like a life of labor, if you ask me. Maybe she is the wind, and I am the wings.

During several of my spin cycles, when I was being pressured to deliver "fruit," I would yell out loud that the numbers mattered, and the timing was not mine. The timing was set because we are in a numerical wormhole circling, doing the same thing over and over … ad nauseam, I might add. Everything is rearranged in a new mosaic each cycle, but it is the same story again and again! I was home alone as I screamed that the numbers mattered, knowing somebody was listening. They weren't comprehending or they would have stopped pressuring me to deliver before my time, but they heard me.

The numbers all matter;	I tried to tell them.
Why don't they believe me?	I promise it adds up!
The dates count:	They are a message.
Don't you see—	Who we are meant to be!

09.11.91.10.28.97.09.24.93.09.29.59.11.11.66.02.09.67.09.24.95.09.07.64.02.07.64
1.3.5.7.9.11.13.33.66

I recently found my baptismal certificate and discovered that I was baptized three days after Buck was born, and I was born three months before Buck. The raising of the temple in three days, me being baptized three days after Buck was born, and my connection to him all these years later simply cannot be a coincidence. But three days in Heaven's time is not the same as in earthly time. It will be seven years between the day I stood before Jesus in Spirit and 2020 when my exile is supposed to be over. It's a long damn time. I could endure almost anything for three days, but 33 years is ridiculous ... I guess I am enduring because I am not dead yet, but I am definitely not having fun. This is not how life should be. The powers in the heavens keep telling me to smile, be cheerful, and don't be a baby; I believe they want to make themselves feel better about what they are doing to me. But I don't appreciate anybody telling me to be cheerful or smile while doing this heinous job—it sucks. I would like to suggest they do the job themselves for as long as I have before they tell me how to feel or be.

Anyway, during our next phone conversation, I told Buck that our birthdates and baptismal dates made sense to me, and he agreed. He even pointed out that my mom's maiden name was used on my birth certificate, which I assumed was a clue. I proceeded to tell him that I believed I was made for him and he was made for me, but that he was simply too stupid in college to see we were two halves of the same whole. He withdrew quickly once again and ended the phone call. I was becoming accustomed to these abrupt endings to our conversations. I even told Buck in my next email that he had mastered the skill of cutting me off in his midlife.

I could carry on with how birthdates and numbers add up to make sense of my life, the Bible, the past, the present, and the future, but I am going to stop here. I have decided to trade in numbers, calculating, and figures for words, writing, and speaking. After all, residing inside my head and trying to figure things out is exhausting and isolating. Silence has gotten me nowhere. I will speak my truth instead.

I have a voice—why not use it?

To give a human example, brethren: no one annuls even a man's will, or adds to it, once it has been ratified. Now the promises were made to Abraham and to his offspring. It does not say, "And to his offspring's," referring to many; but, referring to one, "and to your offspring," which is Christ. This is what I mean: the law, which came four hundred and thirty years afterward, does not annul a covenant previously ratified by God, so as to make the promise void. For if the inheritance is by the law, it is no longer by promise; but God gave it to Abraham by promise. Why then the law? It was added because of transgressions, till the offspring should come to whom the promise had been made; and it was ordained by angels through an intermediary. Now an intermediary implies more than one, but God is one.

—Galatians 3:15–20

Complete

58 A Mosaic—Rearrange the Pieces

Mosaic

But God came to Abimelek in a dream one night and said to him, "You are as good as dead because of the woman you have taken; she is a married woman." Now Abimelek had not gone near her, so he said, "Lord, will you destroy an innocent nation? Did he not say to me, 'She is my sister,' and didn't she also say, 'He is my brother?' I have done this with a clear conscience and clean hands." Then God said to him in the dream, "Yes, I know you did this with a clear conscience, and so I have kept you from sinning against me. That is why I did not let you touch her. Now return the man's wife, for he is a prophet, and he will pray for you and you will live. But if you do not return her, you may be sure that you and all who belong to you will die."
—Genesis 20:3-7

I read this Scripture one morning in the fall of 2018, and it became clear to me that Charles was literally walking me home—back to Buck. After all, Buck was my first husband, and clearly a prophet based on our connection through time and space. (*Now return the man's wife, for he is a prophet …*) Charles, most certainly, is innocent (*Lord, will you destroy an innocent nation?*), not understanding when a marriage starts, just as so many others currently living in ignorance.

The part of the Scripture referring to not touching me I didn't entirely understand but surmised it must have to do with my spirit leaving me after Buck tossed me aside—in other words, me not being "all there" when I married Charles.

With all my talk about Buck over the past few years, it would have made sense for Charles to be angry with me and tell me he wanted a divorce. But he wasn't. In fact, it was just the opposite. He reminded me about friends who divorced and remarried later in life. And while he was telling me those stories, he would roll his wedding band around on his finger; it felt like he was hinting that I needed to be the one to initiate the divorce. Why Charles and I couldn't have a direct conversation, I don't know. It felt to me like we both knew that our marriage was over, but neither of us wanted to pull the trigger. We had a beautiful life together, amazing sons, and great memories. How do you let go of something so wonderful? How does a powerful union of so many years turn into such a mess?

Finally, one fall afternoon when the Spirit was flowing through me, I worked up the courage to tell Charles that the marriage was over and asked him to move out. I wish I had some dramatic story to go with this moment, but I don't. Charles packed his bags and just left. There was an unspoken understanding at this point that we were both working toward the same end goals and that this was a part of the insane process. The end goal being happiness and peace for all of humanity.

Suddenly, I had a feeling of not belonging to anyone for once. Buck was married to someone else, and I was on my own now. A feeling of relief swept through me. Freedom, in fact—in an instant, I didn't have anyone on earth to answer to. I was exhilarated and decided to go on a road trip. I packed a bag and planned a trip down memory lane. I wanted to go back to Toledo, Ohio, where I was born, and visit my mom and dad's gravesites. I hadn't been there in years. Then head to Erie, Pennsylvania, where Buck and I met, maybe stopping at our old college campus in Pittsburgh, and see Niagara Falls before heading to see my girlfriends in Philadelphia.

I decided to start with a weekend of rest in Charleston before heading out on my trip down memory lane. Well, I thought it was going to be rest. It turned out to be exhausting. I arrived in Charleston knowing that a hurricane was heading that way in a few days. I arrived at my hotel and discovered that it was almost empty. People were starting to flee days before the hurricane. I had that eerie feeling I get when I know I have walked across dimensions because things felt "off."

The skies were sunny, but you could see the dark clouds, the storm rolling in, and the wind was picking up. I decided to go paddleboarding, and surprisingly the adventure rental staff let me go out on Shem Creek. The water was high and encroaching on the parking lot where I hopped on a paddleboard and headed down the creek. It was exhilarating being the only one on the creek with the water level so high, the ocean creatures unsettled, and the skies unusually beautiful with a mix of bright sun and dark storm clouds in the distance moving toward shore. After a short paddle, I headed back to my hotel.

When I arrived at the hotel, it was just me, the hotel staff, and one other woman named Colleen. She and I chatted at the pool that afternoon while we lounged on the pool chairs reading and sipping cocktails. I was unusually relaxed considering the news programs were showing backed-up roads lined with the cars of locals trying to get out of town before the storm hit.

Suddenly, I felt sick. It was odd how quickly the nausea came over me, but I packed up my things and headed up to my hotel room. I made it up the elevator, but on the way down the hall to my room I violently threw up clear liquid everywhere; it was unnatural because I had just eaten lunch while sitting next to the pool. I broke out in a cold sweat and decided I needed some fresh air. I headed back down the elevator and out the front door and then vomited my meal all over the front entryway of the hotel. How strange; I have gotten sick many times over the course of this slow and painful walk through hell, but I have never separated liquids from solids while vomiting. A new talent, I guess. I felt better by the next morning and was glad to be heading on my road trip down memory lane. I wasn't sure exactly what happened in Charleston, but I was certain that it was a part of this otherworldly insanity—my slooooooooooow walk through the fire to squash the antichrist—who without question is in the world as Jesus declared long ago.

I decided to text Buck before I left, letting him know that I wanted to stop and say hello to his parents when I got to Erie if he was agreeable. I was surprised when he indicated that they would love to see me. I didn't expect him to agree to the visit after our last phone call. He seemed annoyed with me during the conversation and cut the call short when I told him that I thought we were made for each other but that he was too stupid to recognize that in college. It also occurred to me that if Buck was truly happily married, why would he let his parents know he was communicating with me after all these years? I chalked up his agreeing to my visiting his parents to the constant conflicting information that the universe was giving me in an effort to detach me from earthly things. My mind circled to the possibility that Buck and his parents were supporting the powers that wanted to grow my temple to completion so they could get the information out of my brain. And if that's the case, at the end of this exile, there is a distinct possibility that Buck will want nothing to do with me but is simply working toward the greater good of the world. And Buck, in fact, would say those exact words to me in a conversation a few weeks later.

I decided to push Buck and the conflicting messages he was giving me out of my mind. The freedom from men was liberating, and maybe I was better off on my own. I felt like I had endured enough torment from many men in my eternity already. My boys were grown, and I had nobody to answer to. I was driving a red convertible with the wind blowing my hair about and music blasting. My goal was to forget the world for a couple of weeks. I was sick and tired of thinking.

My three sons will always be an exception to forgetting men because I raised them, and they are good.

The world needs good men, and I believe I delivered a few.

A Few Good Men

The first stop on my freedom trail was Toledo, Ohio. On my way there, Mary Anne met me in Columbus for lunch. It was not far for her to drive, and I didn't have to veer off my path. We sat and chatted for a couple of hours. I loved seeing Mary Anne because she believed everything I was experiencing. Sometimes, she would suggest alternative conclusions to those I was drawing, which was refreshing—to have someone challenge me. It didn't happen often anymore. People seemed to wait to hear what I saw and thought. And then, when I shared my thoughts and experiences, they would stare at me blankly with no comment or response. It made life quite boring.

I confided in Mary Anne about my predicament of not knowing who I was married to. I hadn't shared my confusion with anyone, but I trusted her guidance and discretion. When I told her about how I had asked Charles to move out of the house, she was surprisingly supportive. In fact, she understood. She reminded me that the Virgin Mary had Joseph to support her, and he had believed her. It made me feel better about my decision. Charles didn't believe in my Spiritual experiences when they were occurring but instead thought I was a mental patient. If I am here to do this job, where is my Joseph?

After lunch, I drove the rest of the way to Toledo and visited my parents' and grandparents' gravesites. I shed tears, which was nice, and fondly revisited old childhood memories. A time when life was simple. Visiting a gravesite has always seemed odd to me because a person's Spirit leaves their body when they die. But it forced me to think about my parents when I hadn't for years. I left flowers at the gravesites and proceeded to my hotel.

On arrival at the hotel, I entered my room and went to brush my teeth. On the back of my hand, I noticed an ash mark that looked like it came from fire, and then a mustard seed rolled off the back of my hand onto the bathroom counter. I wasn't fazed. I was used to miracles happening around me at this point. What kind of a burnt offering had Mary Anne given me? The gift of faith? I felt like I had faith, but maybe she had given me a boost? I hope she didn't suffer on my behalf; I wouldn't ask that of anyone. Had she offered something of herself to support me?

Mary Anne is a fierce warrior for Jesus Christ and a strong believer in what I was experiencing. I knew through revelation that the confirmation name I was receiving in Heaven was going to be Mary Anne, after the blessed mother and her mother, Ann. But it is also fitting because Mary Anne provided a powerful start to my seeking Jesus Christ and has been supportive along my path.

While in Toledo, I had dinner with my mom's best friend, who was also my dad's second wife. We had a pleasant dinner and caught up on each other's lives. The next morning, I stopped and saw my dad's brother at his place of work. My uncle seemed to be doing well and was getting ready to retire. He was friendly for someone who had decided years ago that my sister and I were a bother. Someone must have clued him in to who I was and what I was experiencing because he said he had heard that I was seriously into my faith journey. I let my anger toward my uncle's abandonment of my sister and me go. He is family, and it was time to move on.

I headed on to Erie to address the thorn in my side. On the drive, I started to mentally rehearse what I might say to Buck's parents. Why had I asked to see them anyway? It was starting to seem silly, but I knew I would follow through and likely say more than I wanted to. The powers in heaven were working hard to "empty" me at this point. I was praying for all my chains to be broken so I could move on with my life no matter what the future held.

As I approached Erie, the roads and other sights became familiar. My mind circled, contemplating why love had to be a triangle; it's a stupid plan if you ask me. Charles is desperately in love with me; why can I not just love him back the same way? It would make more sense. Charles is Spiritually beautiful, he wants me, he is the father of my children, he is deserving of my love, and that is the prayer I sent up to Heaven. Why can't Charles make me tremble the way Buck does? And make me crazy the way Buck does? Not that someone making you crazy should be a good thing, but when it comes to love, it simply is.

I drove past my high school, then stopped at the bridge Buck and I used to park under. I remembered how he used to kiss me, and just thinking about it sent chills down my spine all these years later. We would park for hours and not run out of things to talk about or get tired of making out. Maybe our connection was just a youthful thing that burns out, and I am an idiot.

I drove past the house where I lived during high school—the one my mom died in, the one where the neighbor boy climbed the downspout to knock on my bedroom window, the one where I threw water balloons at my dad from the roof, and the one where Buck crushed his beautiful cheekbone when he ran into a tree. All my trains of thought seemed to end with Buck. It frustrates me.

As I left my old neighborhood and headed toward my hotel in downtown Erie, I began to experience sharp chest pains—seven distinct and sharp pains. I remembered that it was September 15, the feast day of Our Lady of Sorrows, and I realized that, yes, the deepest sorrow of my heart was the loss of Buck—the love I never recovered from. Even though it was the worst chest pain I had ever experienced, I didn't even consider going to the doctor. I was certain the pain was heaven working on emptying me so I could do God's work here on earth. Plus, I thought, if I die today—I will finally rest. Let it be. Besides, I'd had enough of hospitals for one lifetime. What would I tell the doctor anyway? "God is curing me and purifying me while I am alive, so I am feeling the seven sorrows of Mary!" I think not—that would land me in the loony bin in Erie for sure. Nope, not going down that path again.

The chest pain ended after a few minutes, and I continued on my way. I drove downtown to the docks in Erie, and my mind went right to the first time I met Buck. He looked and acted so casual around me. Just like he was acting now—as if I don't really matter to him. Except for the words in that email that said he would or could never love anyone more than he loved me. I pondered that statement and decided that it also meant Buck loved me in the present. If Buck could never love anyone more than he loved me, then he must love me now—right? I told myself frequently that I was right so that this whole fantasy I was having about us was not one-sided. And so I wouldn't feel like a total idiot when I saw Buck's parents.

The next morning, I attended Mass at Saint Matthew's Cathedral in downtown Erie, and a couple of things were "off," which made it clear to me that I was operating in an alternate dimension. First, only five people attended the Mass, and it was conducted in the sacristy. No priest was present, and yet the body and blood of Jesus Christ were served. That would never happen in the Catholic Church. I decided that in this dimension, I must be a priestess, or we would not be breaking bread together. I am the living Spirit in this dimension—wherever I am. My Papa used to say to me, "Wherever you go, there you are." I had no idea what he was talking about until recently. I go places all the time that make no sense and quote Papa—right after reciting the mantra I made up to cast out demons for Jesus. What a bizarre life I am living.

As I was leaving Saint Matthew's Cathedral in Erie, I noticed that the stained-glass window at the very front of the church had Jesus Christ standing at the center and a woman with a halo or host glowing over her head. The woman was sitting on the floor below Jesus with a gold cup covered with a white cloth. I stood staring at the stained glass astounded, confident that the woman was me and that it was my cup of suffering that was set aside. The stained-glass image was identical to my interaction in the upper room a couple of months before when Jesus wouldn't let me pick up my chalice. I determined that I was in a dimension ahead of the time I am from, or maybe catching up to where I was supposed to be. I had never seen a stained-glass window with that image before, and I had been to many Catholic cathedrals.

Later that day, I went to a sports bar in Erie to watch part of the New England Patriots game. Two unusual things happened. First, the bar had ashtrays everywhere, and people were smoking inside. Pennsylvania has a nonsmoking law in public buildings and restaurants. What dimension or time was I in that had people still smoking in restaurants?

While sitting at the bar and watching the game, I was talking with a young man. I sensed he was an angel watching over me or sent to deliver a message. It wasn't the kind of place a woman would go on her own. Anyway, the young man told me that he was working at a prison but was a Navy Reservist and was being deployed to Poland for a year. He hoped upon his return to meet a woman and start a family.

After I left the bar, the song on the car radio was Imagine Dragon's "Radioactive."

The song made me think of what was happening in my life. I was most definitely waking up as I felt my body and brain coming back to life. Maybe I was breaking into Heaven, and if I didn't, I would blow a gasket in my brain soon. I had ash on my hand that morning, and it felt like the Apocalypse. I'd just talked to a kid who worked in a prison. And not only did I emit the perfume of Heaven out of the top of my head like a spouting whale from time to time, but I had lucid dreams and visions of the "New Heavens and a New Earth" in the book of Revelation—the Apocalypse. Everything that day in Erie was making perfect sense to me, which usually meant I was floating in the heavens. I could connect everything to my life.

Crap, I thought to myself, what will happen next?! Go with me for a moment:

I drive to the local grocery store and pick up a box of chocolates called "Absolutely Nuts" and some flowers for Buck's parents. I decide that at the very least, they will get a laugh out of the name of the candy. I pull up and park in the driveway, check in the mirror to see if I am presentable, and worry that I smell like smoke. Even more concerning, I take a deep breath, knowing that I am not in my normal dimension, so I'd better be guarded. Who knows what I might say in this dimension with my mind "flying?"

Buck's mother answers the door. She is an older version of the woman I remember. Petite, full of life and fire; who else could rear nine children successfully?! Buck's dad is more present than I remembered: calm, collected, and Spiritually enlightened. They hug me, and we say some niceties. They mention that Buck let them know that I was having some "Spiritual experiences" that I was interested in sharing with them. Buck's dad had considered becoming a priest prior to meeting Buck's mother, and I was interested to see if he could provide any theological insight regarding my experiences. It crosses my mind that if he had become a priest, I would not be in this pickle.

I sit down on the couch next to Buck's mom. His dad is in a rocker recliner, and I see that his vision is not good. I notice a family picture on the wall right across from me and get up to look. The smile on Buck's face stirs me; damn, I am attracted to him. Buck looked the same as when I saw him six months ago, but something about that smile in the picture disarms me. Our aging aside, I am still drawn to him.

I sit back down on the couch and proceed to do exactly what I did with Buck—and even worse. I tell his parents my whole story and add that I wanted to marry their son but that he decided to move on without me when we finished college. I tell them everything—tears, the whole nine yards. I share that I am annoyed with Buck now because he is not telling me to take a hike. Seriously, shouldn't a happily married man tell an old girlfriend proclaiming to still love him to get lost? "Take a hike" seems like what Buck should be saying to me: I tell his mother this!

They are shockingly supportive of me, interested in my Heavenly experiences, and believe what I am sharing. Buck's dad says the thing he remembers most about our relationship is how upset Buck was when my bird flew out of his apartment window during college. As we are ending the conversation, his mother says that maybe Buck just means that he loved me one way, and now his wife is the love of his life. Suddenly things feel awkward, and I don't want to make her uncomfortable, so I tell her that I was not physically attracted to Buck when I saw him recently, but that I am trying to purge my "issues" so I can move on with God's plan for me. Buck's mom quickly responds, "You mean sexually?" I say yes. And then I make a quick and pleasant exit. I get in my car and drive away, screaming out loud, "Shit, shit, shit!" I am getting nowhere breaking this chain.

The harder I tried to empty myself and rid myself of this attachment to Buck, the more I wanted him. How would I ever do what Jesus Christ is asking me to do? I hate this process.

The following day, on my way to Niagara Falls, my phone rang, and it was Buck. I pulled off the highway and parked under a bridge. He asked me if I was able to see his parents. I paused momentarily, positive that he had already talked to them. There's no way Buck didn't call them to see what I said or that his mother didn't call him to say I broke down crying and was absolutely nuts. But I decided to play his game and told him first about the chocolates, "Absolutely Nuts," I brought his parents. Buck started laughing out loud and then restrained himself to be serious again. I proceeded to tell him that I was very sorry because I unloaded my whole story. I confessed that I was worried that I made his mom uncomfortable. Buck quickly said he must cut our conversation short and call to check on his parents. I was left hanging ... again. I thought to myself, *where can I find a rope and a beam?* And then I laughed at myself, knowing I would never do that because I couldn't risk not seeing Jesus Christ. The one who died for me, the one who has wooed me and made me feel loved, the one who penetrated through the world to show me his love. I will march on to do his work and wait for eternal love—earthly love is too painful.

I prayed later that day and asked Jesus when my suffering would stop. *What exactly is your plan for me?* I need to know. I was not supposed to get weary, but I was. Jesus responded with a voice in my head, saying, "Amy, my love, my plan is for you to be strong, fearless, and mine." This response renewed me—at least for the moment.

As I was leaving Erie to continue my journey, I heard a voice in my mind telling me to get off at Exit 29 for gas. I looked up at the road signs and saw that I was at Exit 13 and assumed Exit 29 would be a little way down the road. The voice in my head said, "No, it's the next exit, I promise. Get off the highway for gas at Exit 29 because I need to fix you." I knew it was Buck talking in my head.

In fact, I was quite certain that Buck was across the street from his parents' house when I was visiting them by the way his mom flashed the porch lights on and off when I left. I decided to play Buck's game and pulled off at Exit 29, which did turn out to be the very next exit. And as I was pumping gas, I experienced the tightness across the top of my intestines that frequently occurred. Was Buck fixing my insides? Or was this part of the "work" we were doing? Honestly, nothing would surprise me anymore.

My mind quickly jumped to considering the numbers of the two exits on the highway. Buck is associated with 13 because he was born in '67, and Charles is associated with 29 because he was born on September 29. So, I pondered, did I get off at a stop along my journey and live an entire lifetime with Charles so Buck could fix me?

No, that would be insane.

Both Charles and Buck are 11's—maybe I needed two men to do my job since my birthdate is 11/11/66. Buck's birthdate is 2/9/67, so my spinning mind calculated that he is an 11 (2+9=11), which means he goes with me. And Buck is a 13, which for me is Heaven. Charles was born on 9/29/59, with 9 being the number of Christ's perfection, and 2+9=11. So, using my logic, if Charles is perfection, then my heart is confused. The other possibility is that Charles is a 9/11—you know, an emergency, because Buck was a dumbass and tossed me aside. I circled and concluded that Charles and Buck were both fixing me. Buck is the voice in my head and the one who holds my heart, and Charles is Christ's perfection. I'm sure I could have sliced and diced this a few more ways, but I stopped.

Connecting so many things that appear random seems insane. I can see why people look askance at how I am pulling things together. Honestly, I have questioned my own sanity on more than one occasion. But when the insanity of connecting what appear to be unrelated occurrences and numbers leads to being able to find a way to connect absolutely every single thing back to the whole, one lands at **COMPLETE SANITY**.

Labyrinth

59 I'm Every Woman

Mary   Judah

                                        Garden

Woman   Holy   Virgin   Red
        Tomb
        Sarah   Saint   Arm   Omega   Scattered
    Sea   First   Faithful   Above   Miriam
Mother
Underground   Candle   Daughter   intuitive
Rose
            Sister   Prophetess   harlot   Love   Pieces
        Fire   Gospel   Eleven   Loyal
            Theresa   Trodden   Scattered   Promised   Lady
    Frozen   Ark   Predicted   Disciple   Prayer
            Delphic   Heaven   Believed   Intelligent
Migdal   Seven   Undervalued   Resurrected
Light
            Past   Bathsheba   Isaiah   Answer   Zion
Deborah   Magdalene   Powerful   Everything   Fearless
        Judge   Frozen   All   Warrior   sinner
            Angel   Rock   Confident   Epic   New
    Exiled   Below   Forgiven   Earth
Darkness   Tree   Apostle   Cornerstone   Covenant
Scorpion   Strong   Veteran   Mouthpiece   Wise   Beloved
        Last   True   Valued   Whole
                                Woman
            R   U

                        Amy

The Woman and the Dragon

A great sign appeared in the sky, a woman clothed with the sun, with the moon under her feet, and on her head a crown of twelve stars. She was with child and wailed aloud in pain as she labored to give birth. Then another sign appeared in the sky; it was a huge red dragon, with seven heads and ten horns, and on its heads were seven diadems. Its tail swept away a third of the stars in the sky and hurled them down to the earth. Then the dragon stood before the woman about to give birth, to devour her child when she gave birth. She gave birth to a son, a male child, destined to rule all the nations with an iron rod. Her child was caught up to God and his throne. The woman herself fled into the desert where she had a place prepared by God, that there she might be taken care of for twelve hundred and sixty days.

—Revelation 12:1-6

Beloved

Beloved

As my view of Heaven came into focus, I was able to fit my life into almost every story about a woman in Scripture. For starters, Jesus addresses "Beloved" throughout Scripture, which is what Jesus calls me in the upper room of my mind, making me his beloved. In addition, my name is Amy, which means beloved.

Daughters Jerusalem

I can easily make the events of my sister's and my life fit with Daughters Jerusalem. Why would Jesus say in Luke 23 that Daughters Jerusalem should weep for themselves and their children, not for Jesus? Because Jesus understood when marriage began and that women were committing adultery and covered in sin. Not only that, I continually hear the universe telling me that I am "forever green." Why would so many saints and angels have to come to resurrect me if I am a seasoned veteran? Unless the game of life is so ruthless, and I was held underground so long, or maybe I simply refused to play a game of life. My grandmother's name was Ruth, and while I loved her, she broke my heart when she died and gifted my nieces her jewelry while I inherited the gold Lady Liberty twenty-dollar coin of Papa's—a ruthless way to season a girl into a woman if you ask me.

> *But Jesus turning to them said, Daughters of Jerusalem, do not weep for me, but weep for yourselves and for your children. For behold, the days are coming when they will say, "Blessed are the barren, and the wombs that never bore, and the breasts that never nursed!" Then they will begin to say to the mountains, "Fall on us;" and to the hills, "Cover us." For if they do this when the wood is green, what will happen when the wood is dry?*
> —Luke 23: 28 – 31

Samaritan Woman

I can transform myself into the Samaritan woman at the well, being a blood relative who helps Jesus complete the job of collecting the sheep and getting them through the gate into the Kingdom. Providing the world with clean water also happens to be a passion of mine. Jesus says to the Samaritan Woman, *"for you have had five husbands, and the one you have now is not your husband. What you have said is true!"* (John 4:18)— I can connect this scripture to myself in three ways:

I had more husbands than I realized due to the misunderstanding over when a marriage started, I have been confused about who I was married to as I spun in circles, and most importantly, **WHAT I SAY IS TRUE!**

Bathsheba

I was Bathsheba when I got in the jet tub with Buck to cleanse him after he dirtied me up by tossing me aside: *"It happened, late one afternoon, when David rose from his couch and was walking about on the roof of the king's house, that he saw from the roof a woman bathing; the woman was very beautiful."* (2 Samuel 11:2). It has crossed my mind that if Buck had me get off at exit 29 to spend an entire lifetime with Charles so I could be fixed, then metaphorically he "killed" Charles—in the sense that Charles's temple was likely laid bare handling the "spiritual traffic" that surrounded me. Charles was sent to Egypt to resurrect me and then lose me at the end. Now that sucks as far as a story goes, let alone the fact that this is a real-life story.

Mary

Next, the repeated visions I had of being at the base of the cross trying to catch Jesus's blood and Jesus telling me that I was there with him would be a compelling indication that I was "Mary." There were only a few women at the cross, and they were all named Mary. It makes me wonder if everyone back then had the same name or if we are in a time loop, a game of life, and history is repeating the same story.

Mary Magdalene

Buck tossed me aside, which landed me as Mary Magdalene, a harlot, with seven husbands. Mary Magdalene was in a cave in Egypt and locked out of the Promised Land. Jesus looked down from the Promised Land before his crucifixion and Mary Magdalene was underground in a cave. They were circling one another but were never on the same plane of existence, standing face to face. One right side up and one upside down. And Buck and I never seem able to find one another; it's as if we are operating in opposite realms or dimensions. When I looked at Scripture, it became clear that we are trying to evolve Humanity or more directly end an idiotic game of life that devolved humanity.

In a passage from the *New American Bible*, Mary of Magdala **bent over into** the tomb—she bends down into the tomb and then **turns around** later, not recognizing Jesus. Mary Magdala does not ascend to "Heaven," reaching the Promised Land or the "temple" (dome) in her brain. She remained in Egypt. When you turn around on a flat plane or in Egypt, you are just spinning in circles or looking at your reflection. How does that song go? Climbed a mountain and I turned around to see my reflection ...

The Appearance to Mary of Magdala

But Mary stayed outside the tomb weeping. And as she wept, she bent over into the tomb and saw two angels in white sitting there, one at the head and one at the feet where the body of Jesus had been. And they said to her, "Woman, why are you weeping?" She said to them, "They have taken my Lord, and I don't know where they laid him." When she had said this, she turned around and saw Jesus there, but did not know it was Jesus. Jesus said to her, "Woman, why are you weeping? Whom are you looking for?" She thought it was the gardener and said to him, "Sir, if you carried him away, tell me where you laid him, and I will take him." Jesus said to her, "Mary!" She turned and said to him in Hebrew, "Rabbouni," which means Teacher.
—John 20:11-16

In the Revised Standard Version of the Bible, "Woman" is evolving because now Mary Magdala **stood** outside the tomb to **look** in. Note that Mary does not bend down or get in the tomb now, but stands up and does not go back in. Also, Mary, instead of turning around to look at her reflection in the mirror, turns **round**, clearly indicating that Mary has now left the cave, left Egypt, and has traveled to the Promised Land, entering God's temple in her head. She now rises on top of time and looks down from above. She is no longer spinning in circles because she is alive in God's Kingdom.

Jesus Appears to Mary Magdalene

But Mary stood weeping outside the tomb, and as she wept she stooped to look into the tomb; and she saw two angels in white, sitting where the body of Jesus had lain, one

at the head and one at the feet. They said to her, "Woman, why are you weeping?" She said to them, "Because they have taken away my Lord, and I do not know where they have laid him." Saying this, she turned round and saw Jesus standing, but she did not know that it was Jesus. Jesus said to her, "Woman, why are you weeping? Whom do you seek?" Supposing him to be the gardener, she said to him, "Sir, if you have carried him away, tell me where you have laid him, and I will take him away." Jesus said to her, "Mary." She turned and said to him in Hebrew, "Rab-bo'ni!" (which means Teacher).
—John 20:11

Okay, there are several other women in the Bible, and if I think about it enough, I can make everything circle back to me by connecting the women in the Bible to someone in my life or connecting them to me, but let's move on.

60 The Teacher Becomes the Student

Dream

I arrive at the upper room, and Jesus is at the door. I smile because Jesus hadn't been waiting at the door for quite some time now. I look down at his feet, and the buckets of water and sponges were there. Jesus motions that I should wash his feet. I wash His right foot, then stand up and look at Him. Jesus kneels and washes my right foot, and then when he stands up, he grabs my waist and switches places with me. Now Jesus is at the door, and I am standing inside the upper room. Jesus lays his two hands against my two hands, and we lean our foreheads against one another. Then Jesus gets down and washes my left foot, stands up, and I get down and wash his left foot. When Jesus stands up, he puts his hands on my neck and massages the lump in my throat three times. I take a big swallow each time and feel something release. When Jesus finishes, he looks up at me, and I grin and ask him if he would like to come in and sit on my couch. Jesus smiles, grabs my hand, and we walk over to the couch and sit down. I feel the butterflies in my stomach and the chills move from my core outward, blanketing my body in warmth. Jesus smiles, knowing what he does to me, liking it.

I compose myself, and with a serious expression, ask, "What is on your mind today?" Jesus says, "I need to talk to you about three things." I say, "Okay, go ahead." He continued, "You are definitely without question the sweetest person I have ever met. You are more beautiful now than ever. However, I take issue with number three."

I smile, look at Jesus, and say to him,
"Oh, really. Why is that? It seems that I am the one who invited you into the upper room today, not the other way around."

Jesus grins ear to ear and says,
"Exactly my point. If I remember correctly, my letter at the bottom says, 'The teacher will become the student, and the student will become the teacher.'"

I fight back a smile and laughter and say,
"Let me ponder that and get back to you."

When I woke from the dream, I was utterly convinced that Jesus was now Buck, or Buck was now my Jesus. The three things in my dream were from the email I had sent Buck a few months back, explaining to him that I knew I was talking to him through time and space because he'd often told me when we were kids that I was the sweetest person he had ever met and that I would grow more beautiful with age. Then at the bottom of the letter he'd sent me in college, he wrote that if I became too proficient, the teacher would become the student, and the student would become the teacher. Only Buck could be such a smart ass to say this to me in a lucid dream.

Have my dreams become the dreams of Jesus Christ, and his dreams become mine?

Now before faith came, we were confined under the law, kept under restraint until faith should be revealed. So that the law was our custodian until Christ came, that we might be justified by faith. But now that faith has come, we are no longer under a custodian; for in Christ Jesus you are all sons of God, through faith. For many of you as were baptized into Christ have put on Christ. There is neither Jew nor Greek, there is neither slave nor free, there is neither male nor female; for you are all one in Christ Jesus. And if you are Christ's, then you are Abraham's offspring, heirs according to promise.
—Galatians 3:23–29

Face to Face

61 The Kingdom Is Now—East to West

For Zion's sake, I will not be silent, for Jerusalem's sake I will not be quiet until her vindication shines forth like the dawn and her victory like a burning torch. Nations shall behold your vindication, and all kings your glory; You shall be called by a new name pronounced by the mouth of the Lord. You shall be a glorious crown in the hand of the Lord, a royal Diadem held by your God. No more shall men call you forsaken, or your land Desolate, but you shall be my Delight, and your land Espoused. For the Lord delights in you and makes your land his spouse. As a young man marries a virgin, your Builder shall marry you; And as a bridegroom rejoices in his bride so shall your God rejoice in you.
—Isaiah 62:1–5

Buck reminding me in the dream that he had written at the bottom of the letter that the teacher would become the student, and the student would become the teacher, made me think Buck was my Jesus and I was his Mary. But it also reminded me of something Buck said a few months earlier when we spoke on the phone. Buck said, "Amy, you are smarter than that." I don't remember what I said that made Buck respond to me that way, but his comment would eat away at me for months to come.

What exactly is it that I am being stupid about while blindfolded, shackled, and gagged, spinning in circles? And how dare Buck say that to me, when he is the ass who sent me on this ride through hell? I am not living life in a linear timeline, so maybe Buck isn't either because he said to me several months prior, "Amy, we should have listened to you. You were right." What exactly he was saying I was right about, I am not entirely sure. But if I'm right, then why would Buck imply that I was not smart? It seems to me that the only thing I am stupid about is Buck.

Here is what I know for sure. The government and the church don't know everything; in fact, they are wrong about many things. Women are undervalued in this world. Moreover, often, women are the ones with the right answers—pay attention, gentlemen.

I'm not only a loving mother, but I'm smart, I'm funny, and what I want matters. I want to

216

make a difference in the world and let people know that God is love. I'm allowed to express my emotions and say how I feel. People don't have to like it. And that's not my problem; it's theirs.

My body is God's temple, Christ lives in me, and Heaven flows through me. God is love, and with God, everything is possible. Keep Scripture on your lips daily, seek God's Kingdom, and everything you need will be received. When your stars align, everything you need is everything you want. God will reveal meaning through the words on the pages of the Bible—the message God intended your mind to understand.

Live in the Kingdom of God now. Not yesterday or tomorrow, because that is choosing to live in hell. Live in the moment you are in. Most importantly, love, because love is what matters. Love God, love yourself, love your family, love your neighbor, and love your enemy too.

To attempt to explain Heaven in concrete human terms is fruitless. Experiences of Divine origin are specific to that moment in time for the person or people they are being revealed to, for the divine is intentionally drawing each of us into the form that completes our perfection in the grand plan of unification and glory. To think that a Scripture or vision has only one meaning and understanding is childish. God is ever-changing to meet each of our needs to mold us to the Master's plan. God loves that much.

When I stood at the tomb, there were no clothes left behind because I, Amy Jean, a sinful woman, picked them up, put them on, and walked out of the tomb as a whole Woman, complete in Christ, having reached the summit of the tree of life. I stretched from east to west, using my brain.

For this, I was born, and for this, I came into the world—to testify to the truth.

You are the salt of the earth; but if salt has lost its taste, how shall its saltiness be restored? It is no longer good for anything except to be thrown out and trodden under foot by men. You are the light of the world. A city set on a hill cannot be hidden. Nor do men light a lamp and put it under a bushel, but on a stand, and it gives light to all in the house. Let your light so shine before men, that they may see your good works and give glory to your Father who is in heaven.
—Matthew 5:13–16

The cave
had no shadow
no light
darkness surrounds
underground
no rays
to illuminate
decay to
dislodge
stepping into
Light
thick shadows
surround
what gathered
underground
penumbra is heavy
weighing me down
a flatness
cast far ahead
on the ground
no color to display
my rainbow
captured
in my dreams.

Guiding Light

218

62 Empty Plaque

Love bears all things, believes all things, hopes all things, endures all things.
—1 Corinthians 13:7

I was wide awake when I heard a voice in my head; I was straining to hear the words and dimly perceived them through a subtle fog filling my mind. I was able to grasp enough words to piece together Buck saying to me that we are different people now than we were as kids. I supposed he was right, but true love does not fade or dissipate over time—it is eternal, worth risking everything for. So, I wrote Buck a poem for Christmas 2018 ... and even sent it to him:

Empty Plaque

Empty Plaque

An empty plaque
A stolen heart
A missing ring
A harlot with sins of scarlet
A wife tossed aside in youth
Pieces scattered through time and space.

I have stood in time on the other side of Abraham and Sarah and looked right through Isaac, Jacob, and David. I wept with sadness over their sins and breathed in joy over their joys as if they belonged to me. And you were there.

I have telescoped forward hundreds of years from now and turned around to look back and be thanked by women and men for my sacrifices. And you were present.

I floated so far out in the body of Christ that I understood why there were seven raindrops on my windshield, nine ants marching across the picnic blanket, and three leaves falling overhead. And you twirled through my mind.

I sat so high above the world that all people faded into the background of their being, and the unified whole of the Master's plan made perfect sense. And your essence surrounded me.

I had my first career success and wished I could tell you. I lost my dad and glanced around secretly to find you nowhere in sight. Gave birth to my first child and sent you a spark of my joy through the universe. I made some best friends and learned a new dance, then drifted away to try to live without pain. The shock in my spine that closed access to my mind sent me drifting below to an underground cave. I heard you no more, and time passed slowly in this new lonely space.

Our connection now broken, I dreamed our dreams for us. Lost in a song, you became the gold buckle hanging onto my hips at a Florida Georgia Line concert one summer. You were the Buck who made my star shine when you crossed my mind as I drank my latte each day. Our wedding dance was perfect; I'm sorry you missed it. You held me, I trembled, then you twirled me around, and I melted right into your arms. Our home was cozy and mystical, rich in passion and love. We filled it up quickly with family and fun and were loyal and content all the way to the end. Many memories we made—some triumph, some trial—but we embraced each one in sync. We fought, we made up, much laughter, few tears, and great joy and love we found through many amazing years. My secret life helped time pass when loneliness came fast the day I was sent underground.

I took a trip down memory lane to our old stomping ground to gather some pieces, but you were nowhere to be found. Drove the docks where we met when I knew in an instant you were Heaven sent. Saw the tree your face met the day my mom was certain I loved you. And the bridge we parked under when we hid from the world. Stopped to ponder at the beach where we sunbathed the day my mom died; your shoulder I cried on while your arms held me tight. Saw the mailbox you kicked when you thought twice about leaving me behind. The towers we resided in still soar overhead; I avoided the elevator, I'm sure you understand.

When I prayed to God to save me from the isolation that forbade me from living life fully, he threatened to summon you. And in my dream, he did. I took the elevator to Heaven while you climbed the steps. I tried to hide behind the concrete wall I had built in my mind, but you tore it down when I was nowhere to be found. Yet still, you elude me.

I have toiled for hours in daydreams where you stop by to see me just to remind me what it feels like to be ignited. In the middle of the night, your fire sustains me while old memories haunt me as gently you taunt me just out of reach. The chain left unbroken; I cannot escape you. And quite frankly, secretly, I don't want to.

A spark reignited the flame that you started the day you gave me that plaque. I have sunk to the depths of despair and heights high above and now see you again just once more. In my Heaven, you're the buckler who I grab hold of to shield me and protect me when my enemy approaches. You're the one who accepts me when the entire world rejects me. You show up, in the end, to make life seem fair.

As part of spring cleaning, I tried to dream my way to you. But the clock keeps ticking, and time I am losing. So now I have decided to reside in the moment, live my life to the fullest, and stop wandering the universe searching for you. Think I will learn a new dance, sing a new song, make a few more friends, and see more of the world. Attend my sons' weddings and help celebrate their successes. Be the coolest grandma showing up for each moment.

Now my tears they meet oxygen, and my gait has new height. My temple now erected has movement from Heaven as the light of new hope floods my soul. But I since have discovered that thoughts of you hover and won't let me stand with two feet on the ground. I have soared up to Heaven to find I'm a treasure bound up and tethered no more. With my purpose now found, I must find solid ground. Maybe that means we must be unbound?

I would like to tremble when touched, have my heart skip a beat, and find love at my door just once more.

So, if you can't meet me with a response that repeats me, then I must sadly ask,

"May I have my heart back?"

I went to Mass the next day with my temple in full motion. I could feel pressure where a baby's soft spot is on the top of my head. And as I went up to communion, then turned to walk back in my own tracks, I realized that I was emitting the perfume from Heaven. I'm back from Heaven, walking the Earth.

See with what large letters I am writing to you with my own hand. It is those who want to make a good showing in the flesh that would compel you to be circumcised, and only in order that they may not be persecuted for the cross of Christ. For even those who received circumcision do not themselves keep the law, but they desire to have you circumcised that they may glory in your flesh. But far be it from me to glory except in the cross of our Lord Jesus Christ, by which the world has been crucified to me, and I to the world. For neither circumcision counts for anything, nor uncircumcision, but a new creation. Peace and mercy be upon all who walk by this rule, upon the Israel of God. Henceforth let no man trouble me; for I bear on my body the marks of Jesus. The grace of our Lord Jesus Christ be with your spirit brethren, Amen.
—Galatians 6:11–18

THE DISCIPLES SAID TO YESHUA, "WHEN YOU DEPART FROM US, WHO IS TO BE OUR LEADER?" AND YESHUA SAID TO THEM, "I WILL NOT LEAVE YOU ORPHANS. WHEN A FATHER GOES AWAY, IT IS THE MOTHER WHO TENDS THE CHILDREN. ONLY FROM THE TRUTH, I TELL YOU THERE IS ONE AMONGST YOU WHO HAS HAD MY COMMANDMENTS AND KEEPS THEM. THAT IS THE ONE WHO LOVES ME AND IS ALSO LOVED BY ME AND BY THE SPIRIT. TO THAT ONE WILL I REVEAL MYSELF SO THAT YOU WILL KNOW THAT WHAT I HAVE SAID TO YOU IS TRUE, THAT I AM IN THE SPIRIT AS THE SPIRIT IS IN ME. AND THAT SAME ONE WILL THE SPIRIT COMPLETE IN ALL WAYS, SO THAT BY THIS SIGN YOU MAY KNOW MY WORDS ARE TRUE, AND THAT MY TESTIMONY IS OF THE SPIRIT, THE ONE WHO SENT ME."
—Gospel of Mary Magdalene: 35:16–18

What's next:
The Kingdom Has Arrived
Volume 3: Reclaimed

These are the descendants of Noah. Noah was a righteous man, blameless in his generation; Noah walked with God. And Noah had three sons, Shem, Ham, and Japheth. Now the earth was corrupt in God's sight, and the earth was filled with violence. And God saw that the earth was corrupt; for all flesh had corrupted its ways upon the earth. And God said to Noah, "I have determined to make an end of all flesh, for the earth is filled with violence because of them; now I am going to destroy them along with the earth. Make yourself an ark of cypress wood; make rooms in the ark, and cover it inside and out with pitch. This is how you are to make it: the length of the ark three hundred cubits, its width fifty cubits, and its height thirty cubits. Make a roof for the ark, and finish it to a cubit above; and put the door of the ark in its side; make it with lower, second, and third decks. For my part, I am going to bring a flood of waters on the earth, to destroy from under heaven all flesh in which is the breath of life; everything that is on the earth shall die. But I will establish my covenant with you; and you shall come into the ark, you, your sons, your wife, and your sons' wives with you.
—Genesis 6:9-18

It was becoming clear to me that I was playing a diabolical "game of life" rather than living a life. I started to dissect every piece of Scripture I read in an attempt to understand how to solve the puzzle and end the game. I was ready to live a life with what time I had remaining. I knew my temple was in my head and that my mind was undergoing serious restoration so I could gain access to the information in my temple—the ark.

I could feel the cubits as described in Scripture being crunched into my head and little electrical shocks igniting my extremities daily as my body was being brought back to life—a part of the restoration of Lady Zion, I suppose. The transformation of my body got me questioning what exactly the measurement of a cubit was. I Googled cubit one day and discovered that a cubit is a distance from one's elbow to the tip of one's middle finger.

My logical, mathematical mind realized that the distance from a person's elbow to the tip of their middle finger is different for everybody, making the cubit measurement ridiculous from a mathematical perspective but par for the course in this absurd game of life that I am being forced to play. I am assuming that many others are also playing this game—willingly or forcibly, I do not know.

It wasn't long after I Googled the definition of a cubit that I noticed a metallic dot in the joint of my middle finger. And based on what I was piecing together about what was happening in the universe and what had been done to me thus far, I will probably need my middle finger propped up once I face my offenders and my cubit flag starts flying. I will have an "f-you" to express my feeling about what I have endured. No words will be required. A gesture will do.

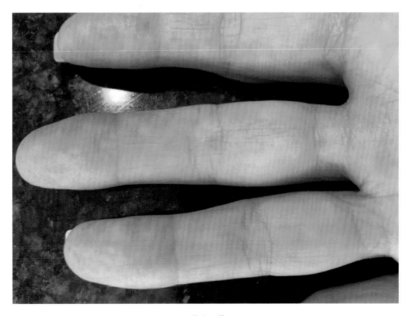

Cubit flag

How humanity got to such a pathetic state, I do not know, but someone recently said to me that boys in groups do stupid things, and I can't argue with that. I have three sons, and they have done some stupid things over the years: Benjamin and his best friend Matthew once decided to see what would happen if they took my china horses and threw them at the window in his bedroom. The china horses and the window broke, of course. Now Ben and Matt were only five or six, so I understand the curiosity and the experiment. But I sent Matt home and made Ben stay in his room until his father got home from work. Those china horses were given to me when I was a little girl by my parents, grandparents, and Nani. I was mad. Too mad to deal with Benjamin's punishment, but I promised him that his father was going to spank him.

When Charles got home, I told him what the boys did and asked him to spank Benjamin. We had never used physical punishment with any of our boys, but I was furious and wanted to be sure Ben understood that what he did was not okay. I stayed downstairs with the younger two boys while Charles went upstairs to deal with Benjamin. I was listening from the bottom of the steps somewhat torn about inflicting physical pain on a child; the horses were just figurines, and I didn't want Charles to hurt Ben—just scare him to make a point.

A minute or two after Charles went upstairs, I heard him roaring laughing—which made me furious. I stormed up the stairs and walked into Ben's room to see Charles laughing so hard that tears were rolling down his cheeks, and Benjamin grinning ear to ear with seven potty training pullups on under his stretched-out pajama bottoms to cushion the blow of the spanking he was anticipating. Yes, I laughed, and we never did spank our boys, but I came damn close one other time.

When we were living in Maine, the boys were six, eight, and ten. Charles and I found a babysitter in the neighborhood. She was sixteen years old, and we were friends with her parents— at least for the time being. Anyway, Christine came to babysit one night, and Charles and I went out on a much needed "date night." We gave the babysitter and boys instructions for dinner and bedtime. When we pulled in the driveway later that evening, the house was dark. I had a bad gut feeling. Charles didn't seem fazed, so I told him to go in, and I would wait in the car to drive the babysitter home since it was dark outside. I sat in the car and waited, and waited, and waited some more. It was taking way too long, so I went into the house to see what was going on.

Well, Charles had the three boys lined up on the couch in the Attic room, and steam was coming out of his head as he scolded them. The babysitter looked distraught, and I could tell she had been crying. I glanced to the right and noticed the double doors of the closet open, and inside was a chair, some ropes, and a bandana sitting on the floor. Apparently, the boys had somehow convinced the babysitter to get in the closet and sit on a chair. They blindfolded her and tied her to the chair. Then they proceeded to close the closet doors! Oh my God, I was horrified. Needless to say, Christina never babysat for us again, and not surprisingly, our friendship with her parents quickly dwindled. Not that I blame them. I would have slinked away from us if the tables were turned.

Somehow, my present life has become a reflection of my past, making me think that I am like the babysitter. I am the one locked up in an exile closet, blindfolded, gagged, and shackled. The big difference is that I am not the babysitter. I am the Mother of all mothers, according to my recent encounters with Heaven, where Jesus informed me that I was the fulfillment of the Prophet Isaiah—the first, the last, and everything in between, Lady Zion…the original seed. Which makes this whole thing bullshit. Excuse my French, but it is bullshit. Holding me in exile for seven years in "the heavens," which is the equivalent of twenty-one years in hell, is an abomination. "The heavens" being the seven dimensions with good and evil spirits fighting over commodities that include material goods, money, youthful looks, health, and time. And what is happening in the universe with people's lives being used as pawns in this multi-dimensional, multi-universal game using real human beings is more than boys in groups doing stupid things.

It's the work of the antichrist.

He shall go out of the house to the doorway and quarantine the house for seven days.
—Leviticus 14:38